Know It, Show It

GRADE 2

Copyright © by Houghton Mifflin Harcourt Publishing Company

All rights reserved. No part of this work may be reproduced or transmitted in any form or by any means, electronic or mechanical, including photocopying or recording, or by any information storage or retrieval system, without the prior written permission of the copyright owner unless such copying is expressly permitted by federal copyright law. Requests for permission to make copies of any part of the work should be submitted through our Permissions website at https://customercare.hmhco.com/contactus/Permissions.html or mailed to Houghton Mifflin Harcourt Publishing Company, Attn: Compliance, 9400 Southpark Center Loop, Orlando, Florida 32819-8647.

Printed in the U.S.A.

ISBN 978-0-358-944645

r4.24

2 3 4 0909 27 26 25 24

4500895620

If you have received these materials as examination copies free of charge, Houghton Mifflin Harcourt Publishing Company retains title to the materials and they may not be resold. Resale of examination copies is strictly prohibited.

Possession of this publication in print format does not entitle users to convert this publication, or any portion of it, into electronic format.

Know It, Show It

Contents

MODULE 1

Week 1 4
Week 2 15
Week 3 25

MODULE 2

Week 1 33
Week 2 44
Week 3 54

MODULE 3

Week 1 62
Week 2 73
Week 3 83

MODULE 4

Week 1 91
Week 2 102
Week 3 112

MODULE 5

Week 1 120
Week 2 131
Week 3 141

MODULE 6

Week 1 149
Week 2 160
Week 3 170

Know It, Show It

MODULE 7

Week 1 178
Week 2 189
Week 3 199

MODULE 8

Week 1 207
Week 2 218
Week 3 228

MODULE 9

Week 1 236
Week 2 247
Week 3 257

MODULE 10

Week 1 265
Week 2 276
Week 3 286

MODULE 11

Week 1 294
Week 2 299
Week 3 304

MODULE 12

Week 1 309
Week 2 314
Week 3 319

Name _____

Closed Syllables

Words with closed syllables usually have a short vowel sound. The word *mat* is a closed syllable word.

▶ Read the words. Three words name things that are alike. Write the word that does not belong.

1. yak   pig   ox   mat   _____
2. run   sit   jog   six   _____
3. clap   snap   grab   bun   _____
4. wet   hat   cap   wig   _____
5. rug   bin   bag   box   _____
6. dog   jet   van   bus   _____

Closed Syllable Exceptions

Sometimes, a word looks like it should follow the closed syllable pattern, but the vowel actually makes the long vowel sound. These words are called closed syllable exceptions. These words have a vowel followed by a consonant like other closed syllables, but the vowel does not have the short vowel sound.

▶ Complete each sentence. Use each word from the box once.

Word Bank

post   jolt   find   gold   wild   cold

1. I get on the bus at the _____ .

2. We had to _____ the lost cat.

3. Dan and Pam go dig for _____ .

4. I put on a hat if it is _____ .

5. Tim is a _____ cat.

6. I sat up in a _____ at the big thud!

Name _____

Open and Closed Syllables

The word *go* is an open syllable word. It has a long vowel sound.

The word *got* is a closed syllable word. It has a short vowel sound.

The word *gold* is a closed syllable exception word. It looks like it should have a short vowel sound, but has a long vowel sound.

▶ Write each word in the correct column.

Word Bank

go	job	hi	bolt	most
jet	me	cab	we	no
find	kind	cold	win	bus

Words with open syllables	Words with closed syllables	Words with closed syllable exceptions
_____	_____	_____
_____	_____	_____
_____	_____	_____
_____	_____	_____
_____	_____	_____

Name _____

Irregular Words

Read and Spell

Read and spell this word to be a better reader.

📖 Read it.

into

👆 Tap the sounds.

◯ ◯ ◯ ◯ ◯ ◯ ◯

✏️ Color it by sound.

into

✏️ Write it.

_____

✏️ Write it again.

_____

📖 Read it.

Mom puts Cam into a crib.

I got into bed.

✏️ Write it in a sentence.

_____

_____

Grade 2
© Houghton Mifflin Harcourt Publishing Company. All rights reserved.

7

Module 1 • Week 1

Name _____

Irregular Words

Read and Spell

Read and spell this word to be a better reader.

📖 Read it.

two

👆 Tap the sounds.

○ ○ ○ ○ ○ ○ ○

✏️ Color it by sound.

two

✏️ Write it.

✏️ Write it again.

📖 Read it.

My sis, Cam, is two.

I get two bins of pens.

✏️ Write it in a sentence.

_____

_____

Grade 2   7a   Module 1 • Week 1

© Houghton Mifflin Harcourt Publishing Company. All rights reserved.

Decodable Text

Name _____

Cam

My sis, Cam, is two.

I see Cam has a bib on.

Cam can sip from a cup and have bits of fig buns.

Mom puts Cam into a crib.

Cam can have a nap on the mat.

▶ Draw a picture that shows what you read in the text.

Name _____

Find the Bits

Dan hid some bits. He hosts a run for kids to find the bits.

"The one who finds the most bits wins," Dan told the kids.

"Get set, go!"

The kids bolt.

They set out to find the bits Dan hid.

▶ Draw a picture that shows what you read in the text.

Name _____

Decodable Text

Tag!

My friends and I love Tag!

"Who wants to be It?" I said.

"Me!" Ben said. "I can be It. Get set to run. And . . . go!"

The two kids run away from Ben, so he can't tag yet.

Ben runs into the hut. He can watch from there.

He sees Meg run by. He runs out of the hut.

"Tag, Meg!" Ben said. "You can be It!"

▶ Draw a picture that shows what you read in the text.

Name _____

Vocabulary

Power Words: Match

Word Bank

| bellowed | bounce | cool | grinned |
| handle | might | munch | rough |

▶ Write the Power Word from *Clark the Shark* that best fits each item.

1. Which word means almost the same as *smiled*? _____

2. Which word names a way to chew food? _____

3. Which word is the opposite of *gentle*? _____

4. This word means *roared* or *yelled*. _____

5. Which word describes how you act in a difficult moment? _____

6. Which word can mean almost the same as *calm*? _____

7. Which word means that you put all your effort into a task? _____

8. Which word names an up-and-down movement? _____

Grade 2

Name _____

Generative Vocabulary

Words That Describe Actions

Verbs are words that **describe actions.** They tell exactly what someone or something is doing.

▶ For each sentence, circle the word that describes an action. Then write an action word from the box that means almost the same as the word you circled. Use a dictionary if you need help.

Word Bank

| dances | drop | gobble | turn | wail | wave |

1. Those toys spin fast.   _____

2. We eat our snacks.   _____

3. The babies cry for their toys.   _____

4. Leaves fall to the ground.   _____

5. The flags flap in the breeze.   _____

6. Maria sways to the music.   _____

Grade 2   Module 1 • Week 1
© Houghton Mifflin Harcourt Publishing Company. All rights reserved.

Name _____

Comprehension

Setting

The **setting** tells where the story happens. It also tells when the story takes place. Understanding why the setting is important will help you understand the story better.

▶ Answer the questions about *Clark the Shark*.

🔍 Pages 18–20 Where do events in the story take place? Why are the changes to the setting important?

_____

_____

_____

🔍 Pages 21–23 Where and when does this part of the story take place? Why do you think the author chose this setting?

_____

_____

_____

_____

_____

_____

Name _____

Vocabulary Strategy

Antonyms

Antonyms are words with opposite meanings. The words *asleep* and **awake** are antonyms.

Word Bank

dark   dirty   found   late   narrow   sour

▶ Read each sentence. Choose the word from the box that means the opposite of the underlined word. Write it on the line.

1. A wide truck drove into a _____ tunnel.

2. I hid the doll and Molly _____ it.

3. He would rather be too early than too _____ .

4. The apple smells sweet but tastes _____ .

5. In the day it is light, but at night it is _____ .

6. Before I washed my clean shirt, it was _____ .

Grade 2
12
Module 1 • Week 1
© Houghton Mifflin Harcourt Publishing Company. All rights reserved.

Name _____

Collaborative Conversations

Follow these rules when you have conversations with classmates or teachers. Circle the rules that are easy for you. Underline the rules that you need to work on.

1. Take turns. When someone makes a point, try to add something to his or her ideas.

2. Speak clearly and be polite.

3. Listen carefully and stay on topic.

4. Ask questions when you don't understand something.

5. Decide if you should use formal or informal language.

Name _____

Speaking and Listening

Have a conversation with a friend about a book you read. Talk about this question:

Do you think others should read this book? Why or why not?

After your conversation, answer the following questions.

Did you take turns?	Yes	No	Sometimes
Did you build on what your partner said?	Yes	No	Sometimes
Did you use complete sentences?	Yes	No	Sometimes
Did you speak loudly and clearly?	Yes	No	Sometimes
Were you polite?	Yes	No	Sometimes
Did you stay on topic?	Yes	No	Sometimes
Did you ask questions?	Yes	No	Sometimes
Did you answer with more than one word?	Yes	No	Sometimes
Did you listen with care?	Yes	No	Sometimes

What rule do you need to practice more?

_____

_____

Phonics

Name _____

The Floss Rule

Some short vowel words end with two, or double, consonants that stand for one sound. For example, the letters *ss* in *kiss* stand for one sound, /s/.

▶ Write the word that best completes each sentence.

Word Bank

jazz
dress
stuff
buzz
hill
fizz
glass
class
sniff
kiss
bell
off

1. Jen has a tan and red _____.

2. Bob can run up the _____.

3. The _____ told us it was the end of class.

4. I love a big _____ band.

5. I have fun in music _____.

6. We have a lot of _____ in the box.

7. I have milk in the _____ cup.

8. The dog gave a _____ of the big bush.

▶ Write two sentences using one of the remaining words from the word bank in each one.

_____

_____

_____

Grade 2   15   Module 1 • Week 2

Name _____

Phonics

Words with -all, -oll, -ull

Word families share the same rime. Some word families include –all, –oll, and –ull. When we see the double consonant *ll* after the vowels *a, o,* or *u*, the *ll* may change the sound of the vowel.

▶ Read the question and look at the picture. Write the word that names the picture.

Is it a **ball** or a **bell**?

_____

Is it **tall** or **small**?

_____

Is it **full** or **fast**?

_____

Is it a **bull** or a **drill**?

_____

Does it **buzz** or **roll**?

_____

Will we **pull** or **tap**?

_____

Irregular Words

Name _____

Read and Spell

Read and spell this word to be a better reader.

📖 Read it. been	👆 Tap the sounds. ◯ ◯ ◯ ◯ ◯ ◯ ◯
✏️ Color it by sound. been	
✏️ Write it. _____	✏️ Write it again. _____

📖 Read it.

It has been fun to see what rolls.

Champ has been the best pet.

✏️ Write it in a sentence.

_____

_____

Grade 2 · © Houghton Mifflin Harcourt Publishing Company. All rights reserved. · Module 1 · Week 2

The Well

Jazz will go to the well to fill his bin.

The well is at the top of a big hill.

Jazz huffs and puffs as he walks up the hill. He fills the bin to the top and lugs it to the log.

Jazz puts the bin by the log. He does not want a mess. Jazz will fill a can to wet the yams by the log.

▶ Draw a picture that shows what you read in the text.

Name _____

Will It Roll?

My friends and I do "Will it roll?"

We set a tall post on a hill. It rolls!

We put a rag at the top of the hill. It does not roll.

"Let us see if a full box will roll," I said. But a box can't roll.

We put a ball at the top of the hill. It rolls!

It has been fun to see what rolls.

▶ Draw a picture that shows what you read in the text.

Name _____

Vocabulary

Power Words: Yes or No?

Word Bank

| panicked | ridiculous | prohibited | cautiously |

▶ Read each sentence. Circle **YES** if the word makes sense or **NO** if it does not. Rewrite the sentence so it makes sense.

1. I **panicked** about the great news.

      YES   NO

_____

2. We laughed at the **ridiculous** joke.

      YES   NO

_____

3. Things that are **prohibited** are against the rules.

      YES   NO

_____

4. It's a bad idea to walk **cautiously** on an icy sidewalk.

      YES   NO

_____

_____

Name _____

Comprehension

Author's Purpose

The **author's purpose** can be to **persuade**, **inform**, or **entertain**. To find the author's purpose, look for clues about the **genre**. You can also ask questions about what you read and find answers.

▶ Answer the questions about *The Great Puppy Invasion*.

🔍 Pages 35–37 What evidence helps you figure out what kind of text this is? Why do you think the author wrote the story?

_____
_____
_____
_____

🔍 Pages 42–46 What is the author's purpose for writing this story? What do you think the author wants readers to learn?

_____
_____
_____
_____

Name _____

Phonics Review

Some short vowel words end with two, or double, consonants that stand for one sound. For example, the letters *ss* in *kiss* stand for one sound.

Word families share the same rime. Some word families include *–all*, *–oll*, *–ull*. When we see the double consonant *ll* after the vowels *a, o,* or *u,* the *ll* may change the sound of the vowel.

▶ Choose a word from the box to complete each sentence.

Word Bank

cliff   fall   dress   grass   buzz   pull

1. I can smell the tulips as I jog in the _____ .

2. The ox can _____ the stuff behind him.

3. I let the bug _____ on my hand.

4. We can go to the top of the _____ .

5. As the sun set, a mist began to _____ .

6. I went with Dad to get a _____ for the ball.

Name _____

Generative Vocabulary

Words That Describe People, Places, Things

Adjectives are words that **describe** people, places, or things. Some adjectives describe how things look, sound, smell, feel, or taste. Adjectives can also describe what something is like or how it acts.

Word Bank

hard   loud   silly   spicy   tall

▶ Complete each sentence with the best adjective from the box. You can look up words you do not know in a dictionary.

1. The mountain is  .

2. I like to watch  clowns.

3. The music is too  .

4. The soup is very  .

5. A snail lives inside of a 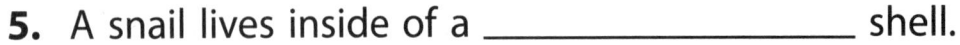 shell.

▶ Choose one of the sentences above. Write other adjectives that can be used to complete the sentence. Use a dictionary to help you.

6. _____

Grade 2   22   Module 1 • Week 2
© Houghton Mifflin Harcourt Publishing Company. All rights reserved.

Name _____

Vocabulary

Power Words: Draw and Write

Word Bank

compliment   elected   local   mock

▶ Draw a picture or write words that will help you remember each Power Word from *Being a Good Citizen*. Try to write more than you draw.

1. compliment

2. elected

3. local

4. mock

Name _____

Comprehension

Author's Purpose

Authors write to **persuade**, **inform**, or **entertain**. How can you find the **author's purpose**? First, look for clues about the genre. Then, ask questions about what you read and find answers.

▶ Answer the questions about *Being a Good Citizen*.

🔍 Page 55 What clues about the genre of this text help you know what type of text you are reading?

_____

_____

_____

_____

🔍 Pages 60–62 What questions were you able to answer about why the author wrote this text? Using all the clues, what do you think is the author's purpose for writing the text?

_____

_____

_____

_____

Name _____

Phonics

Digraphs sh, wh

The word *shed* begins with the **digraph** *sh*. In a digraph, two letters together stand for one sound.

▶ Write two words to complete each sentence.

1. Shep got a _____ of the _____ in his tank.

   fish   shed   whiff   whim

2. Shep went to the pet _____ to get _____ stuff.

   fish   shop   when   silk

3. He got a _____ and a small _____ to go in the tank.

   whiff   shell   ship   crash

4. Shep spent the _____ and left the shop in a _____

   rush   whip   cash   shell

5. _____ Shep was home, he set the _____ in the tank.

   whim   sash   shell   When

6. Shep set the _____ in the tank and _____ the lid.

   ship   whisk   wish   shut

Grade 2   25   Module 1 • Week 3
© Houghton Mifflin Harcourt Publishing Company. All rights reserved.

Name _____

Phonics

Digraphs th, ch

You can spell the /th/ sound with *th*, as in *bath*.
You can spell the /TH/ sound with *th*, as in *than*.
You can spell the /ch/ sound with *ch*, as in *chat*.

▶ Look at each picture and write the correct word from the word bank.

Word Bank

math
chat
chest
chimp
child
bath
sandwich
chill
then
moth
this
that

 _____	 _____
 _____	 _____
 _____	 _____
 _____	_____

▶ Which words did you **not** write? Circle them in the list. Write a sentence for two of the words.

_____

_____

Name _____

Irregular Words

Read and Spell

Read and spell this word to be a better reader.

📖 Read it.

very

👆 Tap the sounds.

◯ ◯ ◯ ◯ ◯ ◯ ◯

✏️ Color it by sound.

very

✏️ Write it.

_____

✏️ Write it again.

_____

📖 Read it.

"Go, Jed!" Tom yells, and Jed runs very fast.

He is very big!

✏️ Write it in a sentence.

_____

_____

Grade 2   27   Module 1 • Week 3

A Great Pet

Josh has cash from Nan.

"I wish to get a pet fish," Josh tells Mom.

"OK," Mom said. "We can dash to the pet shop. It is not shut yet."

They rush to the shop. Josh tells a woman what fish he wants, and she gets it for him.

"I will call him Shep," Josh said.

"Hi, Shep," Mom said to the fish. "I can tell you will be a very fun pet!"

"Yes, he will," Josh said.

▶ Draw a picture that shows what you read in the text.

Jed Is at Bat

When Tom was at bat, he did not hit the ball.
He got an out. He sat by the others.
So, Jed is up at bat. He is a bat whiz!
He whips the bat.
Wham! The bat hits the ball.
"Go, Jed!" Tom yells, and Jed runs very fast.

▶ Draw a picture that shows what you read in the text.

Name _____

Decodable Text

A Bath for Seth

Our dog, Seth, dug in some mud.

We cannot give Seth a bath in our tub. He is very big! He will not fit in that one.

Mom and I go with Seth to the pet shop so he can get a bath.

"They did a great job!" I said.

▶ Draw a picture that shows what you read in the text.

Decodable Text

Name _____

A Chess Set

Chaz and Beth go to the mall.

"This is such a big mall!" Chaz said.

Chaz and Beth walk and chat about what they find in the shops.

"I will get this cat chess set for Chip," Beth said.

"Chip loves cats and chess very much," Chaz said. "So I know he will love that set!"

▶ Draw a picture that shows what you read in the text.

Name _____

Vocabulary

Power Words: Match

Word Bank

| disaster | fiddled | hamper | mood |
| perfect | planned | queasy | scowl |

▶ Write the Power Word from *Picture Day Perfection* that best fits each item.

1. Which word means the opposite of *smile*? _____

2. Which word names a terrible event? _____

3. Which word can mean the opposite of *ruined*? _____

4. You might feel like this when you are sick. _____

5. Which word means almost the same as *prepared*? _____

6. Which word is a place for dirty clothes? _____

7. This word means *jiggled* or *picked at*. _____

8. Which word means *the way you feel*? _____

Name _____

Comprehension

Characters

The **characters** are the people or animals in a story. **External traits** are what we see about them. **Internal traits** are thoughts, words, and feelings.

▶ Answer the questions about *Picture Day Perfection*.

🔍 Pages 73–76 What words would you use to describe the boy? Why did you choose those words?

_____
_____
_____
_____
_____
_____

🔍 Pages 80–81 What is surprising about what happens in this part of the story? What does the boy's reaction tell you about him?

_____
_____
_____
_____

Name _____

Phonics Review

The word *shop* begins with the **digraph** *sh*. In a digraph, two letters together stand for one sound.

▶ Choose a word from the word bank to complete each sentence.

Word Bank

chill   shut   Which   shell   math   with

1. I got a _____ for the fish tank.

2. I will _____ the drink so I can sip it.

3. I can toss the ball _____ my pal.

4. I am the best at _____ in the class.

5. _____ shop is the best to get this in a rush?

6. Can we _____ the lid to the box?

Inflections –ed, –ing

Generative Vocabulary

Add *–ed* to the end of a **verb** to tell about an action in the past. Add *–ing* to the end of a verb to tell about an action that is happening now or that may happen in the future.

▶ Choose the word that best completes each sentence. Write the word on the line. Circle the word(s) in the sentence that tell you when the action happened.

1. Last week, I _____ the ball into the goal.

    kicked   **kicking**

2. Tomorrow I will be _____ with friends.

    played   **playing**

3. When I was little, I _____ the ball with my hands.

    rolled   **rolling**

4. Now I am _____ it from knee to knee!

    bounced   **bouncing**

▶ Choose another verb about a sport or a hobby. On the lines, write the verb in the past, present, and future tense.

5. _____

   _____

Phonics

Name _____

Digraph ck

In a digraph, two letters stand for one sound. The word *chick* ends with the digraph *ck*, /k/. In a digraph, two letters stand for one sound.

▶ Read each incomplete sentence. Write the word from the word bank that best completes each sentence.

Word Bank
milk
neck
ask
deck
truck
kick
bank
rock
desk
black
chick
trick

1. Dad has a big _____. _____

2. I went to the _____ to get cash. _____

3. The teacher sat at her _____. _____

4. The frog sat on the _____. _____

5. We stand on the _____ as the sun sets. _____

6. _____ the ball to me. _____

7. The van is _____. _____

8. I put _____ in my glass _____

9. The small _____ fits in my hand. _____

▶ Write a sentence for each of the words you did not use.

_____

_____

Grade 2
© Houghton Mifflin Harcourt Publishing Company. All rights reserved.

Module 2 • Week 1

Phonics

Name _____

Digraphs *ng, ph*

In a digraph, two letters stand for one sound.
The digraph *ng* makes the /ŋ/ sound.
The digraph *ph* makes the /f/ sound.

▶ Write two words to complete each sentence.

1. I can _____ a

   _____ to the small chick.

       skunk   duck   song   sing

2. Phil and _____ sit on a

   _____ .

       swing   peck   skill   Steph

3. The duck has a _____ neck and small

   _____ .

       snack   wings   rung   long

4. Steph _____ the bell and

   _____ the drum in the band.

       bangs   rings   sticks   blocks

5. We add a _____ of the class to the dot

   _____ on the wall.

       checks   chicks   photo   graph

Name _____

Phonics Review

In digraphs, two letters stand for one sound.

The digraph *ck* makes the /k/ sound.

The digraph *ng* makes the /ŋ/ sound.

The digraph *ph* makes the /f/ sound.

▶ Write the word that names the picture.

_____

_____

_____

_____

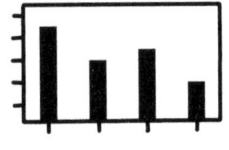 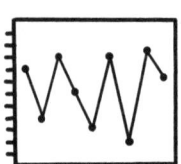

_____

_____

Name _____

Irregular Words

Read and Spell

Read and spell this word to be a better reader.

 Read it. nothing	 Tap the sounds. ○ ○ ○ ○ ○ ○ ○

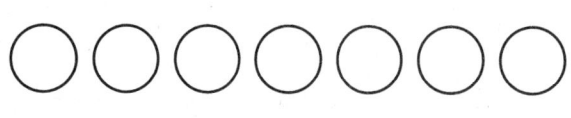 Color it by sound.

✏️ Write it. _____	✏️ Write it again. _____

📖 Read it.

Mack has red socks that have nothing but ducks on them.
I wish that we will have nothing but luck today.

✏️ Write it in a sentence.

_____

_____

The Red Sock

Mack has red socks that have nothing but ducks on them.

He told Dad that the socks give him luck when he kicks the ball.

Today, Mack has on one of the red socks. He can't find the other one.

"Do you know where my sock is?" Mack said to Dad.

Dad picks up the wash sack. He checks the sack.

"You are in luck!" Dad said. "I see your sock. I will put it in the wash for you."

"Great!" Mack said. "I can kick the ball again!"

▶ Draw a picture that shows what you read in the text.

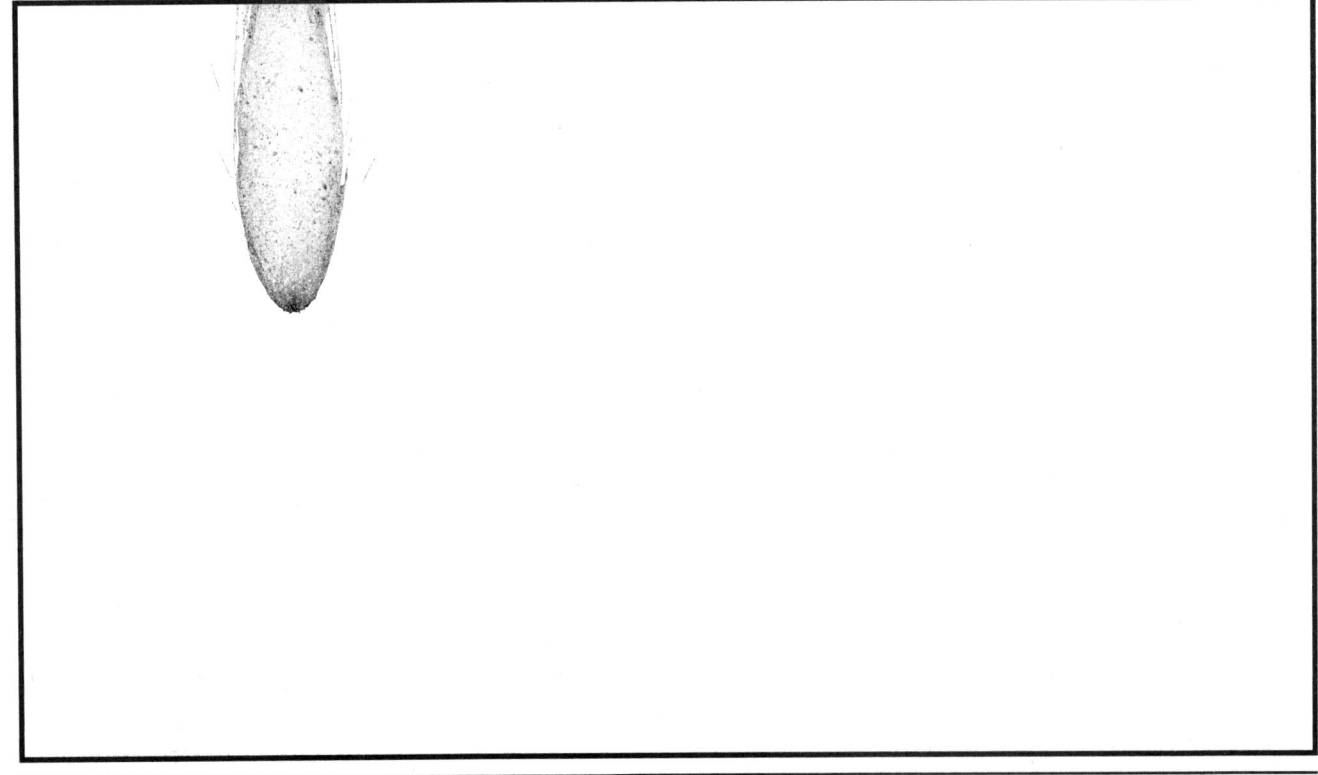

Name _____

Decodable Text

The Class Song

The class will build a song. All the kids get to do a bit.

Tish sings the song.

Jan bangs a gong.

Thad rings two bells.

Chen does the song on a sax.

Miss Sam sings the song with the kids.

It is a very fun song!

▶ Draw a picture that shows what you read in the text.

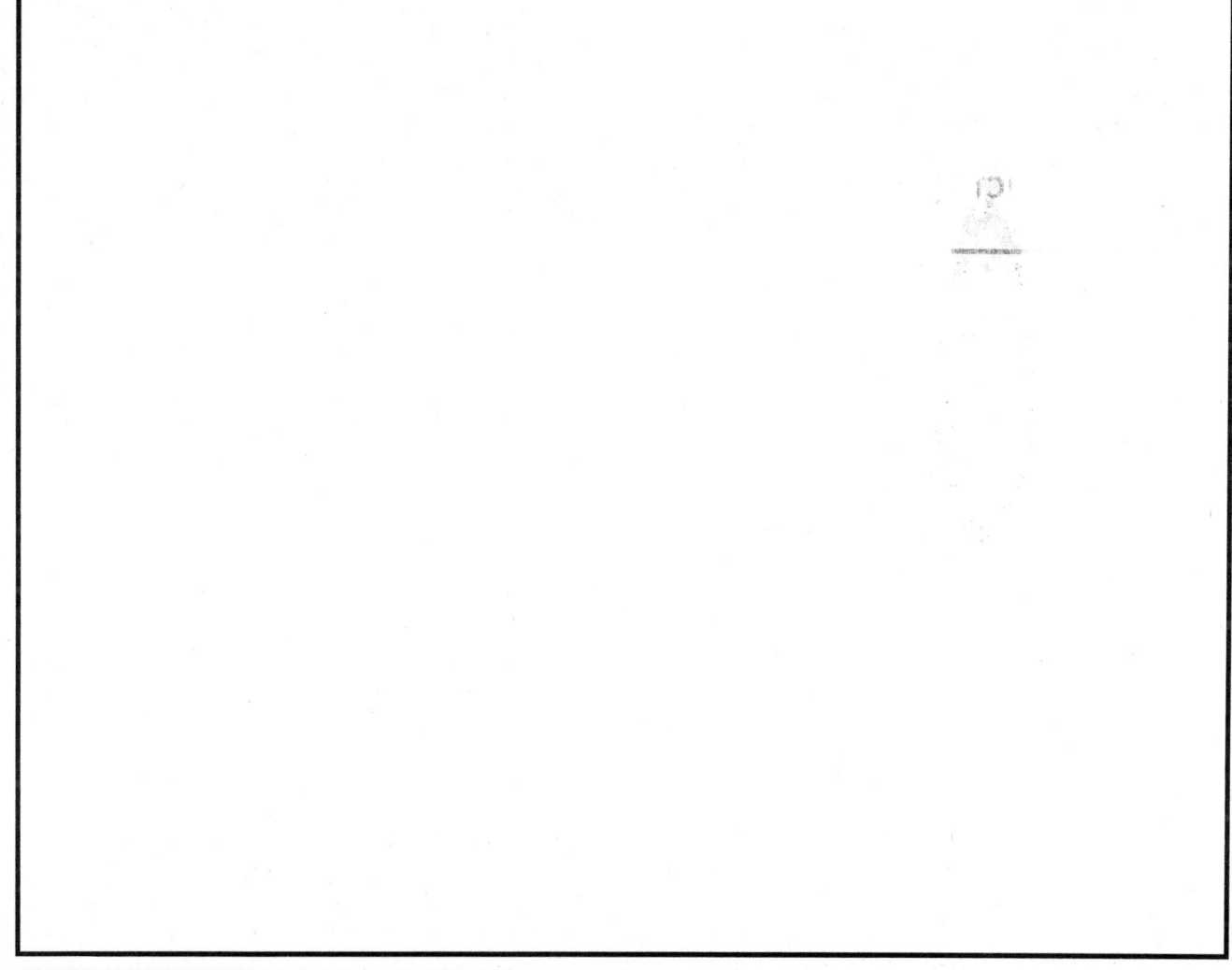

Phil Has a Wish

Phil and Mom will go to the dock to fish.

Phil walks to the shed.

He gets the bin that hangs on the wall. Then he packs chum for fish into the bin.

Mom gets the other things they will lug to the dock.

"Are you all set to go?" Mom said.

"Yes!" Phil said. "I wish that we will have nothing but luck today. We will get lots of big fish!"

"That's a great wish!" Mom said. "Let us go see what we can get."

▶ Draw a picture that shows what you read in the text.

Vocabulary

Name _____

Power Words: Match

Word Bank

amount	easily	example	forms
material	planet	space	tasty

▶ Write the Power Word from *Many Kinds of Matter* that best fits each item.

1. Which word describes how you do something that is not too hard? _____

2. Which word describes Earth? _____

3. Which word describes your favorite food? _____

4. Which word describes what something is made from? _____

5. Which word means almost the same as *an open area*? _____

6. Which word tells how much there is of something? _____

7. Which word describes shapes you can see or make? _____

8. This word is used to explain how one thing is part of a group. _____

Name _____

Generative Vocabulary

Suffixes −er, −est

A **suffix** is a word part added to the end of a base word that changes the meaning of the word. The suffix −er means "more." Add −er to the end of an **adjective**, or describing word, to compare two things. The suffix −est means "most." Add −est to compare three or more things.

▶ Add −er and −est to the base word to make two new words. Write the new words on the lines. Tell a partner what each word means and how you would use it.

1. clean _____   _____

2. nice _____   _____

▶ Choose the word from the box that completes the sentence. Write the word on the line.

Word Bank

bigger   longest   neatest   sweeter

3. That is the _____ piece of string that I have ever seen!

4. My dog is _____ than your puppy.

5. You have the _____ desk in the classroom.

6. I think this apple tastes _____ than that apple.

Grade 2   39   Module 2 • Week 1

Name _____

Comprehension

Content-Area Words

Informational texts often use words from science and social studies to tell about a topic. Readers can use **context clues** to figure out a word's meaning. Context clues are the words and sentences around an unknown word that can be clues to its meaning.

▶ Answer the questions about *Many Kinds of Matter*.

🔍 Pages 104–106   How are all solids the same?

_____

_____

_____

_____

🔍 Pages 114–115   Underline the sentences where *evaporation* and *condensation* are first used. Which word in each sentence is a clue to the meanings of *evaporation* and *condensation*?

_____

_____

_____

_____

Name _____

Vocabulary Strategy

Synonyms

Synonyms are words that mean the same or almost the same thing. *Happy* and *glad* are examples of synonyms.

Word Bank

beautiful   dull   little   silent   tune

▶ Read each sentence. Identify the word from the box that means the same or almost the same as the underlined word. Write it on the line.

1. Let's sing a <u>song</u> together. _____

2. It was <u>quiet</u> in the library. _____

3. I thought the movie was <u>boring</u>. _____

4. The flowers in Nell's garden are <u>pretty</u>. _____

5. Do you want to hold this <u>tiny</u> kitten? _____

▶ Choose one of the sentences above. Explain its meaning. Then on the lines below, write new synonyms for the underlined word.

6. _____

_____

Grade 2   41   Module 2 • Week 1

Name _____

Research

Select a Topic

Follow these steps to select a topic.

1. Brainstorm topics that interest you.

2. Choose three topics. Pick ones that interest you the most.

3. For each topic, list what you already know. Then select a topic.

▶ **Writing Prompt:** Look outside. What are you most curious about?

1. Brainstorm topics about the prompt.

  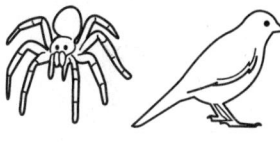

   Possible Topics

   1. _____ 4. _____

   2. _____ 5. _____

   3. _____ 6. _____

2. Choose three topics that interest you the most.

   1. _____

   2. _____

   3. _____

Grade 2
42
Module 2 • Week 1
© Houghton Mifflin Harcourt Publishing Company. All rights reserved.

Research

Name _____

3. Write your three topics in the chart below. For each of the topics, list what you already know. Then select a topic.

TOPICS	1.	2.	3.
WHAT I ALREADY KNOW			

My final topic is _____.

Name _____

Three-Consonant Blends

The word *scrap* begins with three consonant letters. It is a three-consonant blend. You say and blend each consonant sound closely together to read the word.

▶ Look at the picture and read the question. Write the answer.

Is it a **spring** or a **string**?  _____	Do you use it to **drink** or **sprint**?  _____
Do you use it to **scrub** or **strum**? 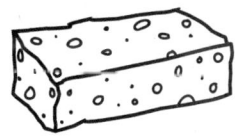 _____	Is it a **scroll** or a **strand**?  _____
Is it a **script** or a **strap**?  _____	Is she **strong** or **slick**?  _____

Phonics

Name _____

Three-Consonant Blends with Digraphs

Sometimes, a consonant blend can include a digraph. Sometimes this means that even though we see three letters, we may only hear two sounds, like in *thr–*, *shr–*, or *–nch*.

The three-consonant blend *squ–* spells three sounds /s/ /k/ /w/.

▶ Read each clue. Unscramble the grapheme cards. Write the word correctly on the line.

Word Bank

squid   thrill   shred   strong   thrust   shrimp   pinch

1. grab a bit of skin   [ch] [p] [n] [i]   _____

2. can lift big things   [ng] [s] [t] [o] [r]   _____

3. It has ink and 8 legs   [d] [i] [s] [qu]   _____

4. A rush of fun   [ll] [th] [i] [r]   _____

5. A small shellfish   [p] [r] [i] [sh] [m]   _____

6. rip up in bits   [r] [d] [e] [sh]   _____

Grade 2   45   Module 2 • Week 2

Name _____

Irregular Words

Read and Spell

Read and spell this word to be a better reader.

📖 Read it.

about

👆 Tap the sounds.

○ ○ ○ ○ ○ ○ ○

✏️ Color it by sound.

about

✏️ Write it.

_____

✏️ Write it again.

_____

📖 Read it.

They'll be at the grass pit at about two.

I sang a song about cats and dogs.

✏️ Write it in a sentence.

_____

_____

Grade 2 — 46 — Module 2 • Week 2

Irregular Words

Name _____

Read and Spell

Read and spell this word to be a better reader.

📖 Read it.

around

👆 Tap the sounds.

○ ○ ○ ○ ○ ○ ○

✏️ Color it by sound.

around

✏️ Write it.

✏️ Write it again.

📖 Read it.

Cass and Meg go for a stroll around the block.

Seth thrusts the sled around to him.

✏️ Write it in a sentence.

Grade 2 — 46a — Module 2 • Week 2

Name _____

Irregular Words

Read and Spell

Read and spell this word to be a better reader.

📖 Read it.

away

👆 Tap the sounds.

○ ○ ○ ○ ○ ○ ○

✏️ Color it by sound.

✏️ Write it.

_____

✏️ Write it again.

_____

📖 Read it.

"I've been away," Nash said.

I will scrub away the mess.

✏️ Write it in a sentence.

_____

_____

A Stroll in Spring

It is spring. Cass and Meg go for a stroll around the block.

They smell fresh grass, and they see buds on plants.

They spot a wet pit in the path. "Should we hop by it or sprint into it?" Cass asks.

"Sprint into it!" Meg said.

They sprint into the pit. It has mud in it.

Cass said, "I got mud on my pants."

"Don't stress," Meg said. "We can scrub them when we get back. The mud will come out."

"I'm glad," Cass said. "Today has been so fun! I do not want mud to mess it up."

▶ Draw a picture that shows what you read in the text.

Name _____

Decodable Text

On the Sled

Jess and Seth go to the big hill. They bring a sled with them.

Jess and Seth squish onto the sled and slip to the end of the hill.

"What a thrill!" Jess said.

"That was the best!" Seth said.

They sled again and again.

Then they stop to have lunch. They sit on a bench by a shrub, and they watch other kids go on the hill.

"Should we go again?" Jess said with a shrug.

Seth thrusts the sled around to him. "Yes! We should sled as much as we can."

▶ Draw a picture that shows what you read in the text.

Name _____

Decodable Text

We'll Have Fun

The bell rang. Chad sprang up from the rug. "I'll get it!" he said as he went to the door.

It was Nash.

"Hi, Nash. I am glad to see you! Where have you been?"

"I've been away," Nash said. "But I am back for the rest of the break."

"Do you want to go kick a ball around?" Chad said.

"I'd love to," Nash said. "Brock and Jill said they'll be at the grass pit at about two, so we can hang with them."

The friends have fun as they kick the ball and chat.

▶ Draw a picture that shows what you read in the text.

Name _____

Vocabulary

Power Words: Draw and Write

Word Bank

| battleground | feud | frenzy | gasped |

▶ Draw a picture or write words that will help you remember each Power Word from *The Great Fuzz Frenzy.* Try to write more than you draw.

1. battleground

2. feud

3. frenzy

4. gasped

Name _____

Comprehension

Connect Text and Visuals

Visuals can help you understand what the author's words don't say. Illustrations can give you details about the characters, setting, or events in a text. In the same way, the **type**, or printed words, an author uses and where the author places it can show a sequence of events or even which character is talking.

▶ Answer the questions about *The Great Fuzz Frenzy.*

🔍 Page 125 What do you notice about the words *boink*, *thump*, and *rumble* on the left side of the picture? What do these words help you understand?

_____

_____

_____

_____

🔍 Pages 148–149 What happened to Big Bark? Why did this happen? How does the picture help you understand how stealing the fuzz led to this problem?

_____

_____

_____

_____

Grade 2   49   Module 2 • Week 2

Name _____

Phonics

Contractions with *will*, *would*, *have*

A **contraction** is a short form of two words put together. An apostrophe (') takes the place of the letter or letters that are dropped.

I will→I'll   I would→I'd   I have→I've

▶ Put the words together to form a contraction. Write the Spelling Word on the line.

Word Bank

she'll
we'll
I've
we've
I'd
we'd
he'll
he'd
I'll
she'd

1. she + would = _____

2. I + will = _____

3. he + would = _____

4. I + would _____

5. he + will = _____

6. I + have = _____

7. she + will = _____

8. we + have = _____

9. we + would = _____

10. we + will = _____

▶ Pick two contractions. Write a sentence for each one.

_____

_____

Grade 2   50   Module 2 • Week 2
© Houghton Mifflin Harcourt Publishing Company. All rights reserved.

Name _____

Inflections –s, –es

Generative Vocabulary

The endings –s or –es added to the end of a **noun** make it **plural**, or change the number of something. The endings –s or –es added to the end of a **verb** show that an action is happening now, or in the present.

▶ Add –s or –es to the noun or verb in parentheses. Write the new word on the line to complete the sentence.

1. Cam (walk) _____ to school with her friends.

2. Lin threw two (ball) _____ through the basketball hoop.

3. Max moved the (box) _____ into the closet.

4. Alex (ride) _____ her bike across the street.

5. Emma (ask) _____ her teacher for help.

6. I watched two (movie) _____ on Saturday.

7. She (catch) _____ the ball from the pitcher.

8. The dog (eat) _____ everything in its bowl.

Name _____

Vocabulary

Power Words: Yes or No?

Word Bank

| plumes | strokes | tumbling | wisps |

▶ Read each sentence. Circle **YES** if the word makes sense or **NO** if it does not. Rewrite the sentence so it makes sense.

1. **Plumes** of clouds make long and thin shapes.

   YES   NO

   _____

2. Your friend **strokes** his dog in a nice, gentle way.

   YES   NO

   _____

3. Rocks **tumbling** down a hill are still.

   YES   NO

   _____

   _____

4. **Wisps** of smoke look like big, fluffy clouds.

   YES   NO

   _____

Name _____

Comprehension

Elements of Poetry

Poetry is a special kind of writing. Poems have **rhythm,** visual **patterns**, and descriptive language. Some poems are written in **stanzas**. These things make the poem pleasing to the eye and ear.

▶ Answer the questions about *Water Rolls, Water Rises*.

🔍 Pages 162–163 Compare and contrast the settings on pages 162 and 163. How do the words and phrases that the poet chose create two very different settings?

_____
_____
_____
_____
_____

🔍 Pages 170–171 How are the describing words and phrases on page 170 different from those on page 171?

_____
_____
_____
_____

Schwa

The schwa is the most common vowel sound. It usually sounds like short *u* or short *i*. The schwa sound is heard in the unstressed syllable of a word. Any vowel can represent the schwa sound.

The letter *o* in the word *wagon* represents the schwa sound.

▶ Look at each picture. Write the word from the word bank that best fits the picture. Circle the vowel(s) that stands for the schwa sound in each word.

Word Bank

camel
banana
salad
mitten
magnet
children
button
wagon

Schwa

The schwa sound usually sounds like short *u* or short *i*. Any vowel can represent the schwa sound.

The letter *o* in the word *wagon* represents the schwa sound.

Word Bank

festival
silent
album
problem
mitten
lemon
wagon
zebra
bottom
children

▶ Write the word that best completes each sentence.

1. The _____ jumps in the grass.

2. We had music at the _____ .

3. The _____ holds a bunch of old photos.

4. I cut up the _____ to put it in the drink.

5. The bin has a flat _____ .

6. It is _____ as I stroll along the path.

7. I had to get help with the math _____ .

8. I had all the bricks in the _____ so I can pull them.

Irregular Words

Read and Spell

Read and spell this word to be a better reader.

Read it.

women

Tap the sounds.

○ ○ ○ ○ ○ ○ ○

Color it by sound.

Write it.

Write it again.

Read it.

The women went for a stroll.

All the women kick the ball well.

Write it in a sentence.

Irregular Words

Name _____

Read and Spell

Read and spell this word to be a better reader.

📖 Read it.

woman

👆 Tap the sounds.

○○○○○○○

✏️ Color it by sound.

✏️ Write it.

_____

✏️ Write it again.

_____

📖 Read it.

The woman can help me find a job.

I think that woman is the best pick for the festival gig!

✏️ Write it in a sentence.

_____

_____

Grade 2   56a   Module 2 • Week 3

Name _____

Decodable Text

The Skit

Our club will do a skit at the talent event.

"What should we do a skit about?" Ava asks.

"I think we should do a skit about animals," Caleb suggests. "They live in the wild, but they talk as humans do."

"Great idea," I said. "And we should have the animals pack for a trip. They can travel on a ship across the world."

"That will be fun," Ava said. "I will be a zebra."

"OK, I love lions best," Caleb said. "So I will be a lion."

"And I'll be a camel," I said. "I can tell that I pack my things for the trip in my camel humps!"

I think our skit will be a hit at the talent event!

▶ Draw a picture that shows what you read in the text.

Decodable Text

Name _____

A Gift for Dad

Mica wants to give his dad a gift, but he has a problem. He can't pick which gift would be best. So he talks with Mom about his ideas.

"I could get an atlas," he said. "Dad loves to travel and find out about spots around the world."

"Dad would love an atlas," Mom said. "The one he has is from long ago."

"Or I could make an album of all of us and the things we have done."

"That is a great idea as well," Mom said. "I can tell you put a lot of thought into this. What if I get an atlas and you do the album?"

"Yes!" Mica said. "I knew you would know what to do. You always have the best plans."

▶ Draw a picture that shows what you read in the text.

Name _____

Power Words: Match

Word Bank

| ace | agency | business | confidently |
| eagerly | located | mystery | seeps |

▶ Write the Power Word from *The Puddle Puzzle* that best fits each item.

1. Which word means the opposite of *pours out*? _____

2. Which word names a place where people work to help others? _____

3. Which word do you use to tell where something is? _____

4. Which word names something that is unknown or hard to understand? _____

5. Which word describes how you act when you feel sure you can do something well? _____

6. Which word describes how you would act if you really wanted to go to the park? _____

7. Which word describes what happens at a place where people shop? _____

8. Which word means *really good*? _____

Name _____

Elements of Drama

A **drama** is a story acted out by people. The parts of a drama include a **cast of characters**, **dialogue**, the **setting**, **scenes**, and **stage directions**.

▶ Answer the questions about *The Puddle Puzzle.*

🔍 Pages 182–183 What is the purpose of the Cast of Characters and Setting? What is the purpose of the dialogue?

_____

_____

_____

_____

_____

🔍 Pages 186–187 Which characters' actions are described with stage directions? What do you learn about them from the stage directions?

_____

_____

_____

_____

Name _____

Phonics

Phonics Review

The schwa sound usually sounds like short *u* or short *i*. Any vowel can represent the schwa sound.

The letter *o* in the word *wagon* represents the schwa sound.

▶ Choose and write two words to complete each sentence.

1. I had a _____ and a _____ at lunch.

   banana   wagon   button   salad

2. I think the best _____ is a _____ .

   zebra   animal   album   children

3. The _____ was full of photos from the

   _____ .

   camel   festival   magnet   album

4. The red _____ can go on the _____ .

   present   salad   ribbon   animal

5. If I sit in the _____ , I must get a

   _____ on.

   button   wagon   children   helmet

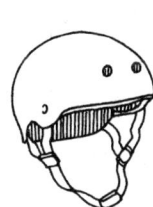

Grade 2   60   Module 2 • Week 3

Name _____

Generative Vocabulary

Words That Name Places

Nouns are words that name people, places, and things. Nouns that name places tell where something is happening.

▶ Choose the word from the box that completes the sentence. Write the word on the line.

Word Bank

closet   home   library   playground   pond   store

1. Dad will buy milk at the _____.

2. Dev forgot his gym sneakers at _____.

3. Tonya saw a big frog near the _____.

4. We must all be quiet at the _____.

5. Please hang your coat in the _____.

6. Tia slid down the slide at the _____.

▶ Find one of the words above in a dictionary. Write the meaning below.

_____

_____

_____

Grade 2
© Houghton Mifflin Harcourt Publishing Company. All rights reserved.

Module 2 • Week 3

Name _____

Phonics

VCe long a and long i

The word *gate* has a **VCe pattern,** vowel-consonant-*e*. In words with a VCe pattern, the first vowel stands for a long sound, and the final *e* is silent.

▶ Complete each sentence. Use each word from the box once.

Word Bank

ate   safe   lake   like   time   wade

1. Dad and Kate went to the _____ .

2. "It is not _____ to dive," said Dad.

3. "We can _____ in," Dad said.

4. Kate and Dad _____ a picnic.

5. "It is _____ to go," Dad said.

6. "I _____ to go to the lake," said Kate.

Grade 2   62   Module 3 • Week 1
© Houghton Mifflin Harcourt Publishing Company. All rights reserved.

Name _____

VCe long u

The word *tube* has a VCe pattern. The final *e* is silent, but it lets you know the first vowel letter stands for a long vowel sound.

▶ Write the words to complete the sentence.

1. _____ takes his _____ to music class.

   tube   Luke   flute

2. Ice is in the shape of a _____, but a glass is in the shape of a _____.

   mute   cube   tube

3. We have a _____ not to be _____ in class.

   rule   duke   rude

4. Can we hum the _____ _____ while we run?

   tune   cute   dude

5. He can _____ the _____ to pull the wagon.

   wagon   use   mule

Name _____

Phonics

VCe long o and long e

The word *note* has a vowel-consonant-e, or **VCe pattern**. In words with a VCe pattern, the first vowel stands for a long vowel sound, and the final *e* is silent.

▶ Complete each sentence. Use each word from the box once.

Word Bank

eve   chose   dome   no   athlete   hole

1. Pete Mole has _____ home.

2. Pete will dig a _____ .

3. On the _____ of his dig, Pete got a lot of rest.

4. Pete has to be strong like an _____ to dig his hole!

5. As Pete digs, he makes a big _____ of sand.

6. Pete likes the spot he _____ to dig his home!

Grade 2   64   Module 3 • Week 1

Irregular Words

Name _____

Read and Spell

Read and spell this word to be a better reader.

📖 Read it. buy	👆 Tap the sounds. ◯ ◯ ◯ ◯ ◯ ◯ ◯
✏️ Color it by sound. buy	
✏️ Write it. _____	✏️ Write it again. _____

📖 Read it.

We buy him a ball.

I had to stop and buy a gift.

✏️ Write it in a sentence.

_____

_____

Irregular Words

Name _____

Read and Spell

Read and spell this word to be a better reader.

📖 Read it.

👆 Tap the sounds.

◯ ◯ ◯ ◯ ◯ ◯ ◯

✏️ Color it by sound.

✏️ Write it.

_____

✏️ Write it again.

_____

📖 Read it.

Our guy Gabe will love this gift.

I can find a guy to fix the pipe by the sink.

✏️ Write it in a sentence.

_____

_____

Grade 2   65a   Module 3 • Week 1
© Houghton Mifflin Harcourt Publishing Company. All rights reserved.

Name _____

Decodable Text

Made by Kate

"Hi, Mike," Kate said. "I made a gift for Gabe."

"That is very kind of you," Mike said. "What is it?"

Kate led Mike to a crate. It had a long and wide shape. She put a hand on the crate.

"It is in this crate. It is a kite for Gabe," Kate said. "I made it with help from our cousin, Jane. Do not tell Gabe!"

"I will not tell," said Mike. "Our guy Gabe will love this gift."

▶ Draw a picture that shows what you read in the text.

A Cake for Duke

"Today is June 3," Mom said. "We should make a cake for Duke!"

Duke is our dog, and we got him on this date a while back.

Duke was so cute and mild that we knew he was the dog for us! He did not pull when we went for a walk, and he could do a lot of tricks.

Mom makes a cake that is safe for a dog. She chops up bits. Then she takes the mix and shapes it into a big cube on a pan. Last, she puts the pan in the oven to bake the cake.

When the cake is done, we give it to Duke. We buy him a ball. And we sing him a tune!

"We love you, Duke!" we sing.

▶ Draw a picture that shows what you read in the text.

Home Late

When Pete got home, Eve was not there. "I hope she did not get stuck," he said.

He put a pan on the stove and got out his phone to call Eve.

But just then, Eve came in the door. "Hi, Pete," she said.

"Hi. I was about to call you," Pete said. "You are late today."

"I had to stop and buy a gift," Eve said. "What is that on the stove?"

"Lemon fish," Pete said. "It will be done in a bit."

"Yum," Eve said. "I'm glad I didn't miss that dish!"

▶ Draw a picture that shows what you read in the text.

Kids' Things

Miss Pike has a box of lost things.

"Hi, class!" she said. "All of the things in this box have been lost by you. I will hold up a thing. Tell me if it is yours."

Miss Pike held up a black hat. The hat was Jack's. It fell off when he was on the slide.

Then Miss Pike held up two red mittens. "I think they are Hope's mittens, but she is not in today." Miss Pike put the mittens on the desk.

"What other kids' things will I pull out?" Miss Pike said.

"Do you see my pet rock?" Cash said.

"Let me see . . ." Miss Pike said. She held up a small white rock. "Is this your rock?"

"Yes, that's mine," Cash said. "I am glad to have it back!"

▶ Draw a picture that shows what you read in the text.

Name _____

Vocabulary

Power Words: Match

Word Bank

greedy   invited   musical   plead
scoots   screams   scurries   shove

▶ Write the Power Word from **Big Red Lollipop** that best fits each item.

1. Which word means that you have been asked to come? _____

2. Which word means *wants more than what is fair*? _____

3. This word describes a pleasant tune. _____

4. Which word means a *hard push*? _____

5. This word is the opposite of *whispers*. _____

6. Which word describes moving with short, fast steps? _____

7. Which word is the opposite of *moves slowly*? _____

8. This word means the same as *beg*. _____

Name _____

Generative Vocabulary

Prefixes un-, re-

The **prefix** un– means "to reverse" or "not." The prefix re– means "again." Use the meaning of the prefix and the **base word** to figure out the meaning of the new word. If you are not sure about the meaning of a base word, use a dictionary.

▶ Add un– or re– to each word. Then write the meaning of the new word on the line.

1. _____ sure   _____

2. _____ true   _____

3. _____ read   _____

4. _____ tell   _____

5. _____ lucky _____

6. _____ write _____

▶ Choose two of the words you made above. Use each in a sentence to show the correct meaning.

_____

_____

_____

Name _____

Comprehension

Point of View

Point of view describes the way readers see things happen in a story. If a story is told from first-person point of view, a character in the story is the narrator. A story told from third-person point of view has an outside narrator.

▶ Answer the questions about *Big Red Lollipop.*

🔍 Pages 208–210 Who is telling the story? What clue in the first sentence on page 208 helps you know?

_____

_____

_____

🔍 Pages 212–215 Who is telling the story now? Is that the same or different as before? What words did you circle that show Rubina is telling the story?

_____

_____

_____

Name _____

Context Clues

When you come to a word you do not know, use **context clues** to figure out what it means. Look around the word you do not know for clues about what it means.

▶ Read each sentence. Circle the clues in the sentence that help you know the meaning of the underlined word. Use the pictures for help, too! Then circle the meaning.

1. The eager children jumped up and down with delight.

   excited   tired

2. A rabbit sleeps in its burrow deep in the ground.

   cage   hole

3. Horses ran around and around the circular track.

   long   round

4. A breeze blew through the tall grass in the meadow.

   field   barn

5. Please discard your trash in the bin outside.

   lift up   throw away

6. Sam felt confident that he did a good job on the test.

   sure   worried

Name _____

Social Communication

During a **social** situation, people use **communication** to exchange ideas with others. **Formal language** is used when following the rules of English. **Informal language** is a style of speaking used with friends and family.

▶ Write two examples for each type of language below.

Formal Language	Informal Language

Name _____

Speaking and Listening

Have a conversation with a friend about *Big Red Lollipop.*
Talk about this question:

**Would you like to have Rubina as a friend?
Why or why not?**

After your conversation, answer the following questions.

Did you use appropriate volume?	Yes	No	Sometimes
Did you speak clearly?	Yes	No	Sometimes
Did you show interest?	Yes	No	Sometimes
Did you nod as you listened?	Yes	No	Sometimes
Did you ask questions?	Yes	No	Sometimes
Did you face your partner?	Yes	No	Sometimes
What language did you use?	Formal	Informal	

What rule do you need to practice more?

_____

_____

Name _____

Phonics

Soft c, Soft g

When the letter *c* is followed by *e, i,* or *y,* it spells the soft *c* sound /s/, like in the word *nice.*

When the letter *g* is followed by *e, i,* or *y,* it can spell the soft *g* sound /j/ like in the word *page.*

▶ Write the word that best completes each sentence.

Word Bank

huge
face
stage
price
nice
page
gist
age
space
change
cent

1. I have five bills and one _____ .

2. I found a _____, red gem on the dig!

3. Gage flips to the next _____ in the script.

4. The cat has a black spot on his _____ .

5. I have to _____ the time on the clock.

6. Can we check the _____ of the doll?

7. The test has a blank _____ I have to fill in.

8. Can I get the _____ of the plot if I skim the tale?

▶ Write a sentence for two of the words in the word bank you did not use.

_____

_____

Grade 2
Module 3 • Week 2

Name _____

Phonics

Trigraphs *tch, dge*

A trigraph is a single sound spelled with three letters.

The trigraph *tch* spells the /ch/ sound, like in *hatch*.

The trigraph *dge* spells the /j/ sound, like in *badge*.

▶ Write the word that best completes each sentence.

1. Mom made a bunch of _____ .

2. I got to watch the chick _____ !

3. We _____ to the flag in class.

4. I will _____ the band so it will fit on the bag.

5. Phil had to _____ the itch on his leg.

6. We ran to _____ the ball.

7. Dad and I camp in a tent but Gram will be in the _____ .

8. I made my lunch in the _____ .

9. The cop let us hold his _____ for a bit.

Word Bank

bridge
stretch
hatch
kitchen
clutch
pledge
badge
fudge
catch
edge
scratch
lodge

Name _____

Decodable Text

Which One?

Mom takes Bruce and Jake to the shop. They see balls and mitts, robot mice, plastic blocks, and a big box in the shape of a rocket. They check the prices. They have some bills and a stack of cents.

Bruce and Jake must pick which thing they can buy with the cash they have.

"We should get these robot mice," Bruce said. "They have such cute faces! And they run, so we can race them."

"I think we should get the rocket box," Jake said. "We can be ace pilots who take off into space!"

"Did you see that there's a sale today?" Mom said. "I think you can get the mice and the rocket box."

"Great!" the kids said.

▶ Draw a picture that shows what you read in the text.

A Red Gem

Men and women dig in the land. They hope to find old items from long ago. They will do tests on the items. The tests can help them know the age of the items and about the place where the items came from.

"Grace, come check this out," Gene said. He held up a huge red gem.

Grace held out a hand to take the gem. "I can tell that once we wipe off this dust and grime, this will be one nice gem. It will shine like it was just bought."

"I hope we can find out a lot about it," Gene said.

"I know," Grace said. "Let us take it back to the lab and see what we can find out!"

▶ Draw a picture that shows what you read in the text.

Decodable Text

Name _____

Stop the Itch

At camp, Madge hikes with the wisdom club. She does work to get an "I Know Plants" badge.

When Madge gets home, she sees red dots on one hand. The dots itch, but she does not want to scratch them.

"I think I have a rash on my hand," Madge tells Mom.

"I see it," Mom said. "I'll get the itch gel from the kitchen. That should help the rash go away."

Mom put the gel on Madge's hand.

"Thanks, Mom," Madge said. "That hit the itch! I think you should get an 'I Always Know What to Do' badge."

▶ Draw a picture that shows what you read in the text.

Name _____

Vocabulary

Power Words: Yes or No?

Word Bank

| argue | blamed | practice | respectful |

▶ Read each sentence. Circle **YES** if the word makes sense or **NO** if it does not. Rewrite the sentence so it makes sense.

1. You don't need to **practice** if you want to play the flute well.

      YES   NO

_____

_____

2. You may **argue** with someone if they **blamed** you for doing something wrong.

      YES   NO

_____

_____

3. "Thank you" are **respectful** words that you can say to someone.

      YES   NO

_____

_____

Name _____

Comprehension

Central Idea

The **topic** of a text is the person or thing that the text is mostly about. The **central idea** is the most important idea about the topic. Readers can use **supporting evidence,** or details, to identify the central idea.

▶ Answer the questions about *Working with Others*.

🔍 Page 233 What is the main topic of the first paragraph? Which details on this page support the central idea?

_____

_____

_____

_____

🔍 Pages 235–238 What is the central idea of this text? Which details support the central idea?

_____

_____

_____

_____

Name _____

Phonics Review

When the letter *c* is followed by *e, i,* or *y,* it spells the soft *c* sound /s/, like in the word *nice.*

When the letter *g* is followed by *e, i,* or *y,* it can spell the soft *g* sound /j/ like in the word *page.*

The trigraph *tch* spells the /ch/ sound, like in *hatch.*

The trigraph *dge* spells the /j/ sound, like in *badge.*

▶ Choose and write two words to complete each sentence.

1. Gage got a _____ and a _____ on his bike when he fell.

    scratch   cent   fudge   smudge

2. We had a bunch of _____ on the _____ to dance!

    stretch   pledge   stage   space

3. I had to duck and _____ to _____ the ball.

    catch   dodge   judge   hatch

4. The _____ made a call on his _____ phone.

    judge   splotch   cell   page

Name _____

Inflections -ed, -ing

Add *-ed* to the end of a **verb** to tell about an action in the past. Add *-ing* to the end of a verb to tell about an action that is happening in the present or that may happen in the future.

▶ Add *-ed* and *-ing* to each verb. Then complete the sentence with the verb that fits.

1. cook _____ _____

    Long ago, Grandma _____ all of my meals.

2. bake _____ _____

    Now we are _____ bread together.

3. help _____ _____

    Grandma _____ me roll the dough.

4. shape _____ _____

    Now I am _____ the dough.

5. wait _____ _____

    We will be _____ for the bread to be ready.

▶ Think of a verb that tells about something you like to do at home. Use the word in a sentence that tells about the past.

_____

Name _____

Vocabulary

Power Words: Draw and Write

Word Bank

booming   persuade   skill   threatening

▶ Draw a picture or write words that will help you remember each Power Word from *Gingerbread for Liberty!* Try to write more than you draw.

1. booming

2. persuade

3. skill

4. threatening

Comprehension

Name _____

Text Organization

Text organization is the way a text is arranged to help readers understand the information. Most texts that tell about a person's life are arranged in **chronological order**. This is the order in which events happened.

▶ Answer the questions about *Gingerbread for Liberty*.

🔍 Pages 246–248 What events happen on pages 246–248? How are these events connected? How are the events organized, and why do you think the author organized the events this way?

_____

_____

_____

_____

🔍 Pages 254–259 In your own words, tell what happens in this part of the text. How does the way the text is organized support the author's purpose for writing it?

_____

_____

_____

_____

Name _____

Phonics

VCe Syllables

A **VCe syllable** is a syllable that has a long vowel sound followed by a consonant and a final silent *e*.

The word *cupcake* has two syllables: *cup-cake*. The first syllable is a closed syllable: *cup*. The second syllable is a VCe syllable: *cake*. In this syllable, *a* spells /ā/ and the final *e* is silent.

▶ Read each word. Then underline the VCe syllable(s) in each word.

pinecone	homemade
pancake	lifetime
athlete	stovetop

▶ Choose and write a word from above to complete each sentence. You will not use all the words.

1. I ate a banana and a _____ when I woke up.

2. I went on the trip of a _____ last spring!

3. Can we name which _____ we think is the best?

4. I can watch my dad make eggs on the _____ .

5. His _____ fudge is the best!

Phonics

Name _____

VCe Syllables

A **VCe syllable** is a syllable that has a long vowel sound followed by a consonant and a final silent *e*, like the second syllable in *cupcake*.

▶ Read each incomplete sentence. Write the word from the word bank that best completes each sentence.

Word Bank

placement
sunshine
cupcake
baseball
lifelong
grapevine
hillside
salute
icebox
reptile
pinhole
athlete

1. We rode the sled up the _____. _____

2. Jen made a _____ to watch the sun.

   _____

3. He has a pet _____ that is in a tank.

   _____

4. I like to stroll in the _____. _____

5. The woman was the best _____ of the time.

   _____

6. Anyone can make a _____ ! _____

7. I place anything cold in the _____.

   _____

8. I think _____ is the best game to watch.

   _____

Grade 2 | 84 | Module 3 • Week 3
© Houghton Mifflin Harcourt Publishing Company. All rights reserved.

Name _____

Irregular Words

Read and Spell

Read and spell this word to be a better reader.

📖 Read it.

anyone

👆 Tap the sounds.

○ ○ ○ ○ ○ ○ ○

✏️ Color it by sound.

anyone

✏️ Write it.

_____

✏️ Write it again.

_____

📖 Read it.

"Anyone want pancakes?" Dad said.

Anyone can take time to be kind.

✏️ Write it in a sentence.

_____

_____

Grade 2   85   Module 3 • Week 3
© Houghton Mifflin Harcourt Publishing Company. All rights reserved.

Irregular Words

Name _____

Read and Spell

Read and spell this word to be a better reader.

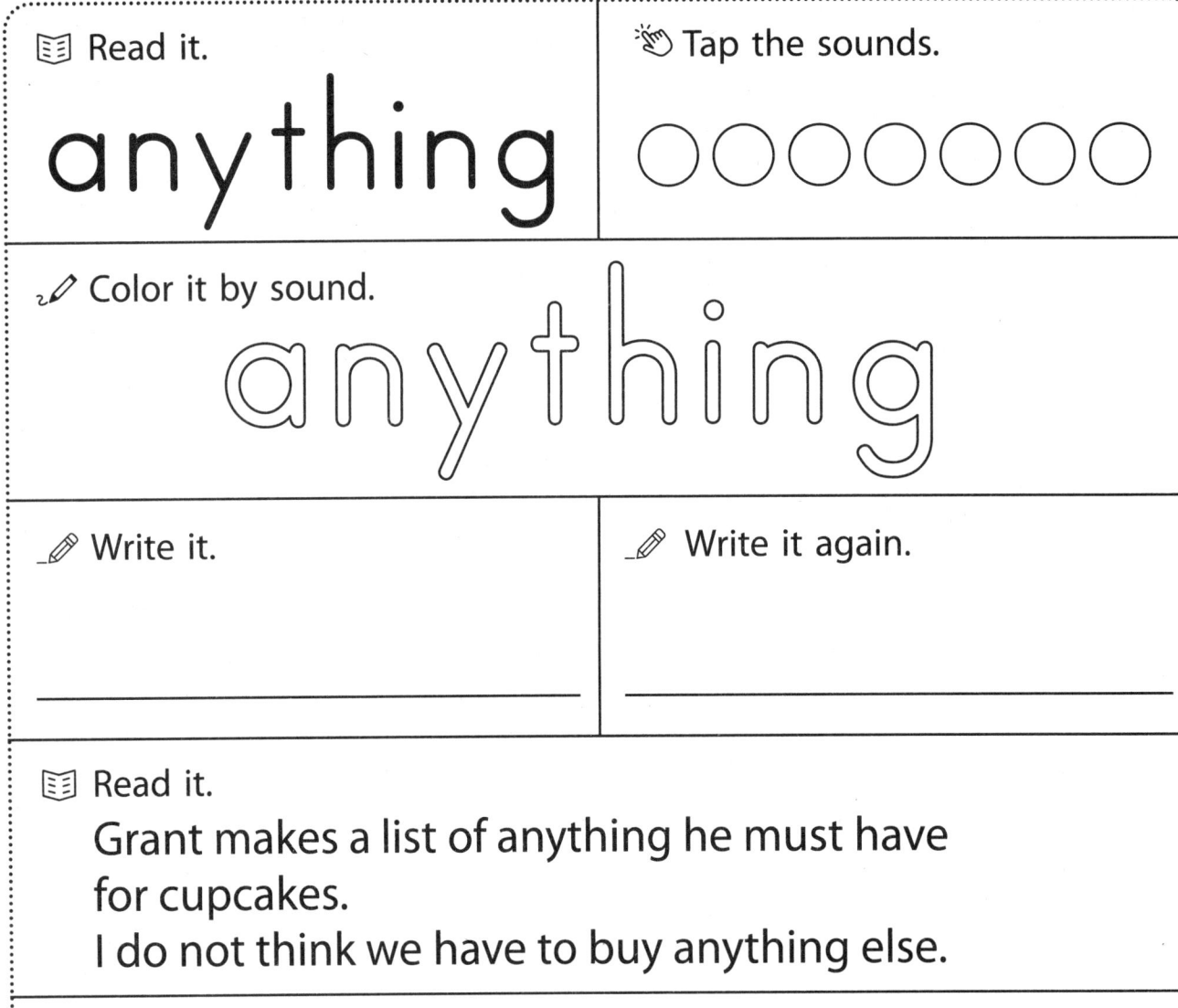

📖 Read it.

Write it in a sentence.

Grade 2   85a   Module 3 • Week 3

Name _____

Decodable Text

Pancakes at Sunrise

The campsite was on a hillside. Mom, Dad, and the kids all slept in a big tent. The sun woke them up, and they left the tent to see the sunrise.

Then Dad set up the camp stove and made pancakes from a homemade pancake mix.

The kids ran around in the golden sunshine until Dad was done.

"Anyone want pancakes?" Dad said.

Mom gave the kids plates with pancakes on them.

"Take your time," Dad said. "These pancakes are hotcakes!"

Mom gave Dad a nudge. "That is such a dad joke!"

Dad said, "Yes, and dads tell great jokes!"

▶ Draw a picture that shows what you read in the text.

Grant's Cupcakes

Grant wants to make homemade pumpkin cupcakes for Mom and Gram.

Grant makes a list of anything he must have for the cupcakes. He does not want to make a mistake. He puts in a bit of this and a bit of that. Then he must mix the bits to combine them.

He puts the mix into a cupcake pan, and Dad helps him put the pan inside the oven.

When Mom and Gram get home, Grant presents the cupcakes he made.

"Thank you, Grant," Mom said. "You are the best!"

"And so are your cupcakes," Gram adds.

▶ Draw a picture that shows what you read in the text.

Name _____

Vocabulary

Power Words: Match

Word Bank

| dragged | excuses | frown | hesitant |
| mumbled | nearby | wrinkled | yanked |

▶ Write the Power Word from *Pepita and the Bully* that best fits each item.

1. Which word means the opposite of *far away*? _____

2. You might act like this when you feel unsure. _____

3. If you did not speak loudly, you spoke like this. _____

4. Which word means the opposite of *smooth*? _____

5. Which word tells how you moved something? _____

6. You might give these for not doing something. _____

7. Which word means *pulled at hard and fast*? _____

8. Which word is the opposite of *smile*? _____

Name _____

Comprehension

Theme

Theme is the **moral**, or lesson, that readers learn from the story. Use these steps to identify the theme: Think about the story's **topic**. Look for the lesson a character learns. Use clues to figure out the message. Explain the theme in your own words.

▶ Answer the questions about *Pepita and the Bully*.

🔍 Pages 268–270 What is this story mostly about? What details in this part of the story help you identify the topic?

_____

_____

_____

🔍 Pages 279–282 What does Pepita realize after she says something mean to Babette? How does this affect the way she tells Babette how she feels about her being a bully? What theme, or lesson, do these details help you figure out?

_____

_____

_____

_____

Name _____

Phonics Review

A **VCe syllable** is a syllable that has a long vowel sound followed by a consonant and a final silent *e,* like the second syllable in *cupcake.*

▶ Choose a word from the box to complete each sentence.

Word Bank

lifespan   lakeside   stockpile   handshake   cupcake   pinecone

1. What is the _____ of a snake?

2. I gave him a nice _____ when I met him.

3. My dad can bake the very best pumpkin _____ .

4. A small _____ fell from the tall branch to the grass.

5. We like to go to the _____ in the spring.

6. Sam has a _____ of a bunch of logs and drinks.

Name _____

Words About Communication

Words about **communication** tell how we share ideas and information. Sometimes we communicate in words. Sometimes we communicate with our faces or bodies. Use a dictionary to look up words you don't know.

▶ Draw a line from the communication words to the correct picture.

1. delighted

2. pleased

Word Bank

giggle   grin   nod

▶ Complete each sentence with the best word from the box.

3. When I meet someone for the first time, I greet them with a big _____ .

4. I _____ at my friend when I agree with what she says.

5. My friend knows that I think his joke is funny because I _____ .

Name _____

Phonics

Inflectional Suffixes -s, -es

When we add the suffixes –s or –es to the end of a singular noun, the noun becomes plural.

We can also add –s or –es to the end of verbs.

We add –s or –es to make the noun and verb agree.

▶ Complete each sentence. Use each word from the word bank once.

Word Bank

| balls | pals | bugs | splashes | benches |
| watches | runs | catches | mittens | |

1. In June, Gage will go for _____ in the sun, while his dog _____ in the lake.

2. In the fall, Gage tosses _____ in the wind, while his dog _____ them.

3. When it is cold, Gage puts on a hat and _____, while his dog sniffs the ice on the _____.

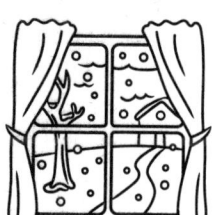

4. In the spring, Gage sits on a bench and _____ his dog chase _____ in the grass.

5. Gage and his dog make the best _____!

Phonics

Inflectional Suffix -ed

When we add –ed to the end of a verb, the verb changes to past tense. This means the action happened in the past.

▶ Write the word that names the action in the picture. Use each word from the word bank once.

Word Bank

smelled   finished   melted   spilled   cracked   landed

I _____ the glass of milk.

The plane _____ on time.

Jill _____ the race.

Meg _____ the rose.

The chick _____ open the egg.

The ice cubes _____.

Name _____

Phonics

Inflections –s, –es, –ed

When we add the suffixes –s or –es to the end of a singular noun, the noun becomes plural.
We can also add –s or –es to the end of verbs.
We add –s or –es to make the noun and verb agree.
When we add –ed to the end of a verb, the verb changes to past tense. This means the action happened in the past.

▶ Add each possible suffix, –s, or –es and –ed to the end of each base word. Then complete each sentence with the correct word.

1. plant _____ _____

   Last spring, we _____ a lot of tulips and bushes along the back fence.

2. watch _____ _____

   I have _____ as the plants have blossomed.

3. pick _____ _____

   Dad _____ some of the tulips and sets them in a vase.

4. bunch _____ _____

   Gage made five _____ of the rose plants to give to his pals.

Grade 2 93 Module 4 • Week 1
© Houghton Mifflin Harcourt Publishing Company. All rights reserved.

Name _____

Irregular Words

Read and Spell

Read and spell this word to be a better reader.

📖 Read it.

says

👆 Tap the sounds.

○ ○ ○ ○ ○ ○ ○

✏️ Color it by sound.

says

✏️ Write it.

✏️ Write it again.

📖 Read it.

Mitch says he likes pancakes!

Mom says she has snacks.

✏️ Write it in a sentence.

Decodable Text

Name _____

Wake Up, Mitch!

The sun was up, but Mitch was not.

"Wake up, Mitch! There are boxes to pack," Mom said. But Mitch did not budge. "Mitch can rest," Dad said.

"I will pack some boxes," Mom said. "You can pack the rugs and lamps. But then Mitch has to wake up and help."

Mom put things in boxes. Dad put the rugs and lamps in the truck.

Mitch was still in bed. So Mom rang bells while Dad sang songs at the top of his lungs.

But once again, Mitch did not budge.

"Mitch says he likes pancakes! I know what to do," Dad said. He got out dishes and pans. Dad made eggs, ham, and pancakes with jam. And the smells woke up Mitch just like that.

▶ Draw a picture that shows what you read in the text.

Name _____

Decodable Text

Basketball

Trish passed the ball to Grace. Grace passed it back with a quick flick. Trish shot the ball and made a basket.

"Nice one, Trish!" Grace yelled. "You crushed it! We should do a pass just like that in the game."

"You've got it!" Trish said as she fist-bumped Grace.

Grace picked up the ball and said, "I think we're done with drills for today. We can go to my home for a snack!"

"That's a great plan!" Trish said. "Mom says she has snacks."

Trish and Grace walked to Grace's home to make a snack.

▶ Draw a picture that shows what you read in the text.

Name _____

Vocabulary

Power Words: Match

Word Bank

| clue | cozy | disturb | pause |
| rattled | sense | steaming | tackled |

▶ Write the Power Word from *How to Read a Story* that best fits each item.

1. Which word describes a place that is warm and nice to be? _____

2. This word means the same as *hint*. _____

3. Which word means *to stop doing something for a short time*? _____

4. Which word means *easy to understand*? _____

5. This word means the same as *pushed to the ground*. _____

6. Which word means the same as *bother*? _____

7. This word can be used to describe a hot bowl of soup. _____

8. Which word is an action that creates noise? _____

Name _____

Generative Vocabulary

Suffixes -ful, -less

A **suffix** is a word part added to the end of a base word that changes the word's meaning. The suffix *-ful* means "full of." The suffix *-less* means "without." Use a dictionary to find the meaning for base words that you do not know.

Word Bank

joy   spot   taste   tree

▶ Read each underlined phrase. Add the suffix *-ful* or *-less* to a word in the box to make a new word that matches the phrase.

1. On my birthday, I am <u>full of joy</u>. _____

2. My cheese sandwich was <u>without taste</u>. _____

3. Mason's clean room looked as if it were <u>without a spot</u>. _____

4. We picnicked in an area that was <u>without trees</u>. _____

▶ Write a sentence for each word.

5. useful _____

6. useless _____

Grade 2   97   Module 4 • Week 1
© Houghton Mifflin Harcourt Publishing Company. All rights reserved.

Name _____

Comprehension

Text Organization

Authors organize texts to fit the topic and their purpose for writing. One way to organize texts is **chronological order**, or in the order instructions should be followed. A **procedural text** gives instructions for how to do something in chronological order.

▶ Answer the questions about *How to Read a Story*.

🔍 Pages 11–15 What do you notice about how the book is organized? How does the organization help you understand why the author wrote the book?

_____
_____
_____
_____
_____

🔍 Pages 18–21 Why do you think the author does not include a heading with each numbered step?

_____
_____
_____
_____

Name _____

Vocabulary Strategy

Multiple-Meaning Words

Multiple-meaning words, or **homographs,** have more than one meaning. You can use **context clues** to figure out the correct meaning.

```
          Word Bank
  park      slide      swing      time
```

▶ Read the story. Complete the sentence with a multiple-meaning word from the box. Underline words in the sentence that helped you know which word to use. Words from the box will be used more than once.

My favorite thing to do with Grandpa is go to the

_____ to play. Grandpa will _____ his car and

then we will walk to the playground. First, Grandpa pushes me

on the _____ . As I _____ higher and higher,

I feel like I can touch the sky. Next, I climb up to the top of the

_____ . I _____ down it really fast and

Grandpa catches me. Finally, it is _____ to

go home. Grandpa and I always have a wonderful

_____ playing together!

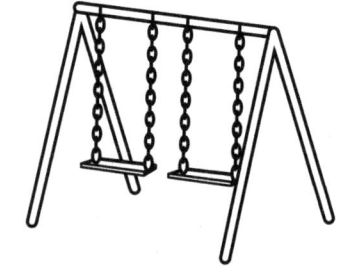

Grade 2

99

Module 4 • Week 1

© Houghton Mifflin Harcourt Publishing Company. All rights reserved.

Name _____

Give and Follow Instructions

Instructions are directions for how to do something. You should give instructions one step at a time. Use **sequence** words like *first*, *next*, and *last* to help explain the order of steps.

▶ Write instructions below for how to choose a story to read. Make sure to use sequence words to explain the order.

_____

_____

_____

_____

_____

_____

_____

_____

_____

_____

Name _____

Speaking and Listening

Give instructions to a partner about your topic:
How to Choose a Story.

After you give instructions, answer the following questions.

Did you speak clearly?	Yes	No	Sometimes
Did you give instructions one step at a time?	Yes	No	Sometimes
Did you tell the steps in order?	Yes	No	Sometimes
Did you use sequence words like *first* and *last*?	Yes	No	Sometimes
Did you repeat the instructions?	Yes	No	Sometimes

Now listen to a partner give instructions about the same topic.

After you listen to instructions, answer the following questions.

Did you listen carefully?	Yes	No	Sometimes
Did you make eye contact?	Yes	No	Sometimes
Did you listen for sequence words?	Yes	No	Sometimes
Did you ask questions if you needed to?	Yes	No	Sometimes
Did you repeat the instructions?	Yes	No	Sometimes

What rule do you need to practice more?

_____

_____

Name _____

Phonics

y as short i /ĭ/

The letter *y* makes the /y/ sound when it is acting as a consonant in a word.

Sometimes, the letter *y* can act as the vowel in the word. One sound the letter *y* can spell when it is acting as a vowel is the short *i* sound, /ĭ/, as in *gym*.

▶ Choose and write the word that answers the clue.

Word Bank

| yelp | myth | system | yak | gym | oxygen |

1. This is a place we can toss balls and jump rope. _____

2. This kind of ox is big and lives in the wild. _____

3. I do this if I smash my hand. _____

4. We have to have this to live. _____

5. This is when a bunch of small things have a role in one big thing. _____

6. This is a kind of tall tale that can have magic. _____

Name _____

Phonics

y as long i /ī/ and long e /ē/

When the letter *y* is at the end of a single-syllable word, it stands for the long *i* sound, as in *sky*.

When the letter *y* is at the end of a multisyllabic word, it usually stands for the long *e* sound, as in *baby*.

▶ Write the word that best completes the sentence.

Word Bank

happy
baby
try
spy
city
cry
sky
candy
fly
dry
plenty
twenty

1. We have _____ of time.

2. I think I can do it if I _____ my best.

3. We watched the plane _____ in the sky.

4. The _____ is in the crib.

5. The song is so sad, it made me _____ !

6. Dean has _____ balls he can toss and catch.

7. We did the game "I _____" to find things at the lake.

8. When something gets wet, we have to let it get

   _____ .

Grade 2 — Module 4 • Week 2
© Houghton Mifflin Harcourt Publishing Company. All rights reserved.

Irregular Words

Name _____

Read and Spell

Read and spell this word to be a better reader.

 Read it.

busy

 Tap the sounds.

○ ○ ○ ○ ○ ○ ○

✏️ Color it by sound.

busy

✏️ Write it.

✏️ Write it again.

 Read it.

Crystal is a busy gymnast.

All the plans we made kept us very busy.

✏️ Write it in a sentence.

_____

_____

Grade 2 — 104 — Module 4 • Week 2

Irregular Words

Name _____

Read and Spell

Read and spell this word to be a better reader.

📖 Read it.

business

👆 Tap the sounds.

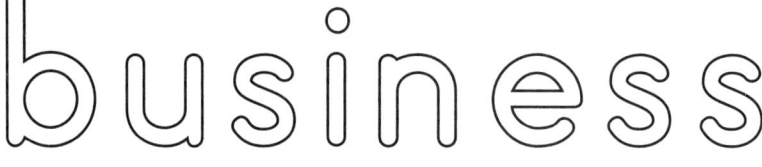

✏️ Color it by sound.

✏️ Write it.

_____

✏️ Write it again.

_____

📖 Read it.

The mice get to business.

It is not my business if he runs at the gym.

✏️ Write it in a sentence.

_____

_____

Grade 2 104a Module 4 • Week 2

Name _____

Decodable Text

Crystal the Gymnast

Can you walk on your hands or do a back flip or tuck jump? Those are typical skills that gymnasts have. Being a gymnast is very fun!

Crystal is a busy gymnast. She is in the gym at sunup. She stretches out with a friend. Then she runs, jumps rope, and does sit-ups.

Crystal likes working on the floor mat the best. She puts on a fast tune. Then she does flips with twists as she passes from one side of the mat to the other.

Today, Crystal and other gymnasts will compete for judges.

The gymnasts who do well will go on to compete at the state level.

Crystal hopes the judges will like what she does!

▶ Draw a picture that shows what you read in the text.

Name _____

Two Shy Mice

Two shy mice stick out of a hole in the wall. They spy on the humans to see if they have left scraps behind. The mice rely on these small bits to live. But they have to watch out for the sly cat who will try to catch them.

One of the mice spots a bit of ham by the kitchen mat. "My plan is to get that ham."

The other sees some bits of a roll by the fridge. "My job is to get those roll bits. Then we can make a sandwich to split."

The mice get to business. They dash into the kitchen and hope that the cat is not about.

In a flash, they go back into the hole and make it home. They split a sandwich and then rest.

▶ Draw a picture that shows what you read in the text.

Name _____

Decodable Text

Windy Lake Ranch

It was sunny out. Dad and Molly drove to Windy Lake Ranch.

Molly wanted to see the pony. The pony's name was Dusty.

"There he is!" Molly said. "Can I ride him?"

It was muddy in the pony ring, but Dusty was happy to give Molly a ride.

Then Molly and Dad went to the rabbit hutch. They could see a rabbit mom and a tiny baby bunny. The bunny was fuzzy and cute, but it could not hop yet.

"The bunny's fuzz looks like sand," Molly said. "I will call it Sandy."

Back at home, Molly told Granny all about the busy time at Windy Lake Ranch and the animals there.

▶ Draw a picture that shows what you read in the text.

Penny's Kite

"Can we go to the inlet today?" Penny asks Mom and Dad. "I want to try out my kite." Penny holds up a pink kite in the shape of a jellyfish.

"OK," Mom and Dad reply.

"We just have to tidy up a bit," Mom tells Penny, "and then we can go."

At the inlet, there is plenty of wind for Penny to fly the kite. But Penny finds that it is tricky business to run in sand and get the kite to go where she wants. The chilly mist from the waves also makes Penny's skin cold and sticky.

"I could fly a kite in gym class," Penny whines, "but that was on grass."

"It's OK, Penny," Dad says. "You did it in gym, but some things take time. Try your best, and you will fly this kite yet!"

▶ Draw a picture that shows what you read in the text.

Name _____

Vocabulary

Power Words: Draw and Write

Word Bank

bind   clever   narrow   plain

▶ Draw a picture or write words that will help you remember each Power Word from *A Crow, a Lion, and a Mouse! Oh, My!* Try to write more than you draw.

1. clever

2. plain

3. narrow

4. bind

Grade 2
106
Module 4 • Week 2
© Houghton Mifflin Harcourt Publishing Company. All rights reserved.

Name _____

Comprehension

Elements of Drama

A **drama** is a story acted out by people. The parts of a drama include a **cast of characters**, **dialogue**, the **setting**, **scenes**, and **stage directions**.

▶ Answer the questions about *A Crow, A Lion, and a Mouse! Oh, My!*

🔍 Pages 32–33 What do the stage directions tell you?

_____
_____
_____

🔍 Page 34 Find details in the dialogue that explain how Crow 1 and Crow 2 are different. How are their perspectives about the pitcher different? How does the setting help you understand what is happening?

_____
_____
_____
_____
_____
_____

Name _____

Phonics

All Jobs of y

The letter *y* makes the /y/ sound when it is acting as a consonant in a word.

Sometimes, the letter *y* can act as the vowel in the word. One sound the letter *y* can make when it is acting as a vowel is the short *i* sound, /ĭ/, as in *gym*.

When the letter *y* is at the end of a single-syllable word, it stands for the long *i* sound, as in *sky*.

When the letter *y* is at the end of a multisyllabic word, it usually stands for the long *e* sound, as in *baby*.

▶ Choose and write the word that completes the sentence.

1. I went to the _____ to find a snack.

   pantry   **baby**   **fly**

2. My mom and dad like to go to the _____ to practice yoga and run laps.

   candy   **gym**   **sky**

3. I will _____ my best to finish the race.

   try   **why**   **city**

4. When I go visit my family, I _____ in a plane.

   myth   **candy**   **fly**

5. I like to make homemade _____ with my Gran.

   candy   **why**   **baby**

Name _____

Generative Vocabulary

Words That Describe People, Places, Things

Adjectives are describing words. They can tell how things look, sound, smell, feel, or taste. They may also tell what a person or thing is like or how they act. If you see an adjective that you do not know, look up the word in the dictionary.

▶ Write words that describe each picture on the lines below. Use a dictionary to help you find interesting adjectives.

		sight	sound	touch	act/is like
1.		_____	_____	_____	_____
2.		sight	smell	touch	taste
		_____	_____	_____	_____
3.		sight	is like	smell	touch
		_____	_____	_____	_____
4.		sight	sound	smell	touch
		_____	_____	_____	_____
5.		sight	sound	touch	act/is like
		_____	_____	_____	_____

Grade 2

Module 4 • Week 2

Name _____

Vocabulary

Power Words: Yes or No?

Word Bank

believe   fulfill   journey   speech

▶ Read each sentence. Circle **YES** if the word makes sense or **NO** if it does not. Rewrite the sentence so it makes sense.

1. If you *believe* something, you think that it is true.

    YES   NO

    _____

2. When you *fulfill* a task, you do not finish it.

    YES   NO

    _____

3. We went on a *journey* from our school to the science museum.

    YES   NO

    _____

4. When you give a *speech,* you only talk to yourself.

    YES   NO

    _____

    _____

Grade 2 — 110 — Module 4 • Week 2
© Houghton Mifflin Harcourt Publishing Company. All rights reserved.

Name _____

Comprehension

Figurative Language

Literal language uses words that mean exactly what they say. **Figurative language** uses words that mean something different from what they say. Two types of figurative language are:

- **simile:** compares two different things using the word *like* or *as*
- **idiom:** words that mean something different from their everyday meaning

▶ Answer the questions about *Hollywood Chicken*.

🔍 **Page 45** Luz tells Chicken Lily that she knows "you will knock their socks off." Is this literal language? Explain why or why not. How might Luz say what she means in a literal way?

_____

_____

_____

_____

🔍 **Pages 46–47** On page 46, what does Chicken Lily compare herself to when answering Luz? Why does she do this?

_____

_____

_____

_____

Grade 2 · 111 · Module 4 • Week 2

Consonant Doubling to add –ed, –ing

When a base word has a short vowel followed by one consonant, double the consonant to add –ed or –ing.

bat + ing = ba**tt**ing   bat + ed = ba**tt**ed

▶ Read each word. Then add –ed and –ing to the end of each word.

1. clap   _____   _____
2. shred   _____   _____
3. run   _____   _____
4. grab   _____   _____
5. stop   _____   _____
6. pin   _____   _____
7. hop   _____   _____
8. scrub   _____   _____
9. sit   _____   _____
10. rub   _____   _____

▶ Choose one word with the suffix –ed and one word with the suffix –ing and write a sentence for each one.

_____
_____

Name _____

Phonics

Consonant Doubling to add −er, −est

When a base word has a short vowel followed by one consonant, double the consonant to add −er or −est.

▶ Read each word. Then add −er or −est to the end of the word to complete the sentence and write the new word in the blank.

1. big   A dump truck is _____ than a bike.

2. hot   It is _____ in the sun than it is in the shade.

3. drum   My mom is a _____ in a rock band.

4. sad   What do you think is the _____ song?

5. thin   A pencil is _____ than a log.

6. big   What is the _____ animal on the planet?

7. fat   My cat is the _____ pet I have.

8. hot   Venus is the _____ planet.

9. skip   Nancy is the best _____ in the class.

10. win   I was the _____ of the game.

Grade 2 113 Module 4 • Week 3
© Houghton Mifflin Harcourt Publishing Company. All rights reserved.

Name _____

Irregular Words

Read and Spell

Read and spell this word to be a better reader.

📖 Read it.

above

👆 Tap the sounds.

○ ○ ○ ○ ○ ○ ○

✏️ Color it by sound.

above

✏️ Write it.

_____

✏️ Write it again.

_____

📖 Read it.

It can jump above all kinds of things!

The plane in the sky is above all the land.

✏️ Write it in a sentence.

_____

_____

Grade 2   114   Module 4 • Week 3

Name _____

Irregular Words

Read and Spell

Read and spell this word to be a better reader.

📖 Read it.

among

👆 Tap the sounds.

○ ○ ○ ○ ○ ○ ○

✏️ Color it by sound.

among

✏️ Write it.

✏️ Write it again.

📖 Read it.

It is nice to be among friends and family.

He was among the best of the batting class.

✏️ Write it in a sentence.

Grade 2 114a Module 4 • Week 3

Name _____

Decodable Text

At the Ice Rink

Ty loves to spend time at the ice rink with friends.

Today, Ty is getting fitted for fresh skates. The old skates he has are cracked and chipping.

Once Ty laces up the skates, he goes out on the ice to skate among friends. He skates fast on the slick ice without slipping.

Ty's friends had been chatting, but they stopped when they spotted Ty's skates.

"Those are nice skates!" Hope said, grinning.

"Thanks!" Ty said. "I'm trying them out today. I think they will help me with my spins."

"That's great!" Eve said. "If you're set to go, we can put on some music and practice our dance act."

"Let's do it!" Ty said.

▶ Draw a picture that shows what you read in the text.

Name _____

Decodable Text

Frogs of All Sizes

Our class takes a trip to the Frog Hut. It is home to all kinds of frogs.

We see a wall of tanks with small frogs inside them. The frogs are vivid shades, and most of them have black spots. One spotted frog is so tiny it can fit on the tip of your pinky.

Next, we see some bigger frogs. One has sticky pads on the end of its legs. The pads help it cling to branches. One other frog has lots of bumps on its skin. The bumps help it blend in with plants.

Last, we see the biggest frog of all. The massive goliath frog is as big as a small dog! It can jump huge distances. It can jump above all kinds of things!

I love seeing all the frogs at the Frog Hut. I hope I can find a job at the Frog Hut when I am bigger.

▶ Draw a picture that shows what you read in the text.

Name _____

Power Words: Match

Word Bank

| beamed | chore | dashed | hobbled |
| jealous | pleasure | superb | thrilled |

▶ Write the Power Word from *If the Shoe Fits: Two Cinderella Stories* that best fits each item.

1. Which word means the opposite of *the very worst*? _____

2. Which word names a feeling of great joy or happiness? _____

3. If you were in a hurry to get somewhere, you did this. _____

4. Which word names a task that someone must do? _____

5. Which word is the opposite of *frowned*? _____

6. Which word is the opposite of *feeling glad for someone*? _____

7. Which word means *walked in a slow and uneven way*? _____

8. Which word describes feeling excited? _____

Name _____

Comprehension

Story Structure

Most stories have the same **story structure**. In the beginning, characters face a **conflict**, or problem. The middle of a story has **events** that happen as characters try to solve the conflict. The events at the end explain the **resolution**, or how the conflict is solved. The conflict, events, and resolution make up the story's **plot**.

▶ Answer the questions about *If the Shoe Fits: Two Cinderella Stories*.

🔍 Pages 61–63 What is the conflict Zoey has? Describe how the conflict is resolved and how the story ends.

_____

_____

_____

_____

🔍 Pages 64–68 Retell the main events of the story. What happens at the beginning? What happens in the middle? What happens at the end?

_____

_____

_____

_____

Consonant Doubling to add -ed, -ing, -er, and -est

When a base word has a short vowel followed by one consonant, double the consonant to add –ed, –ing, –er, and –est.

▶ Read each word. Then add –ed, –ing, –er or –est to the end of the word to complete the sentence and write the new word in the blank.

1. hug   I _____ my dog while we sat on the bench at the vet.

2. flop   I watched as the fish _____ back into the lake.

3. big   Is a golf ball _____ than a basketball?

4. hot   What is the _____ place on the planet?

5. shred   My cat was _____ the napkin into small bits.

6. swim   Is a dolphin a stronger _____ than a human?

7. scrub   My dad was _____ the tile to get it nice and white.

8. drum   I like to be the _____ in my music class.

9. mop   I _____ up the mess I made.

10. fat   The stick I picked up was the _____ of all of them!

Name _____

Generative Vocabulary

Words That Describe Actions

Verbs are words that **describe actions**. They tell exactly what someone or something is doing.

Word Bank

| giggled | pushed | sleeps |
| tumbled | turned | wiped |

▶ Complete each sentence using an action word from the box. Use a dictionary if you need help.

1. My cat _____ next to me at night.

2. The large rock _____ down the grassy hill.

3. Mateo _____ at my silly jokes.

4. Tina _____ the mud off her boots.

5. Chen _____ his little brother on the swing.

6. I _____ around when George tapped my shoulder.

▶ Write a sentence using a verb from the Word Bank.

_____

_____

Grade 2 — Module 4 • Week 3

Name _____

Dropping e for Suffix Addition

When a base word ends in *e*, drop the *e* to add *–ed*, *–er*, or *–ing*.

close – **e** + ed = closed   hide – **e** + ing = hiding

▶ Read each incomplete sentence. Write the word from the word bank that best completes each sentence.

Word Bank

liked
using
riding
chased
diver
making
closed
gamer
baked
hiding
shaker
wiser

1. I watched the _____ jump _____ into the lake.

2. Dad is _____ lunch.   _____

3. I like _____ my bike.   _____

4. Pat _____ the door.   _____

5. Jan is _____ the pen.   _____

6. The dog _____ the cat.   _____

7. Ben _____ a pie.   _____

8. My sis is the best _____ _____ in the club!

▶ Write a sentence for two of the words in the word bank you did not use.

_____

_____

Grade 2 — 120 — Module 5 • Week 1

Name _____

Phonics

Change y to i for Suffix Addition

To add a suffix to a word that ends with a consonant and a *y*, we need to change the final *y* to an *i* before adding the suffix.

try + ed = tr**ied**   try + es = tr**ies**

▶ Read each word. Then add *–ed* and *–es* to the end of each word.

1. cry   _____   _____

2. fry   _____   _____

3. baby   _____   _____

4. candy   _____   _____

▶ Read each word. Then add *–ly* and *–ness* to the end of each word.

5. happy   _____   _____

6. lazy   _____   _____

7. tidy   _____   _____

8. lucky   _____   _____

▶ Choose one word from each section. Write a sentence for each one.

_____

_____

_____

Name _____

Phonics

Spelling Changes for Suffix Addition

When a base word ends in *e,* drop the *e* to add the suffixes *–ed, –er,* and *–ing.*

To add a suffix to a word that ends with a consonant and a *y,* we need to change the final *y* to an *i* before adding a suffix like *–es, –ed, –ly,* or *–ness.*

▶ Read each word. Follow the spelling rules you've learned to add the correct suffix to the end of each word to complete the sentence. Write the new word in the blank.

1. hobby   Singing in a band is one of my _____ I like the best.

2. hike   We went _____ in the hills by the lake.

3. try   He did not win, but he _____ his best at the game.

4. bake   My dad _____ the cake I like best.

5. cry   Sandy _____ when that song comes on.

6. drive   Which _____ is going to win the race?

7. lazy   The cat sat on the bed and _____ licked its lips.

8. happy   Music brings _____ to my life.

9. hope   I am _____ I can find a nice dress for the event.

Irregular Words

Name _____

Read and Spell

Read and spell this word to be a better reader.

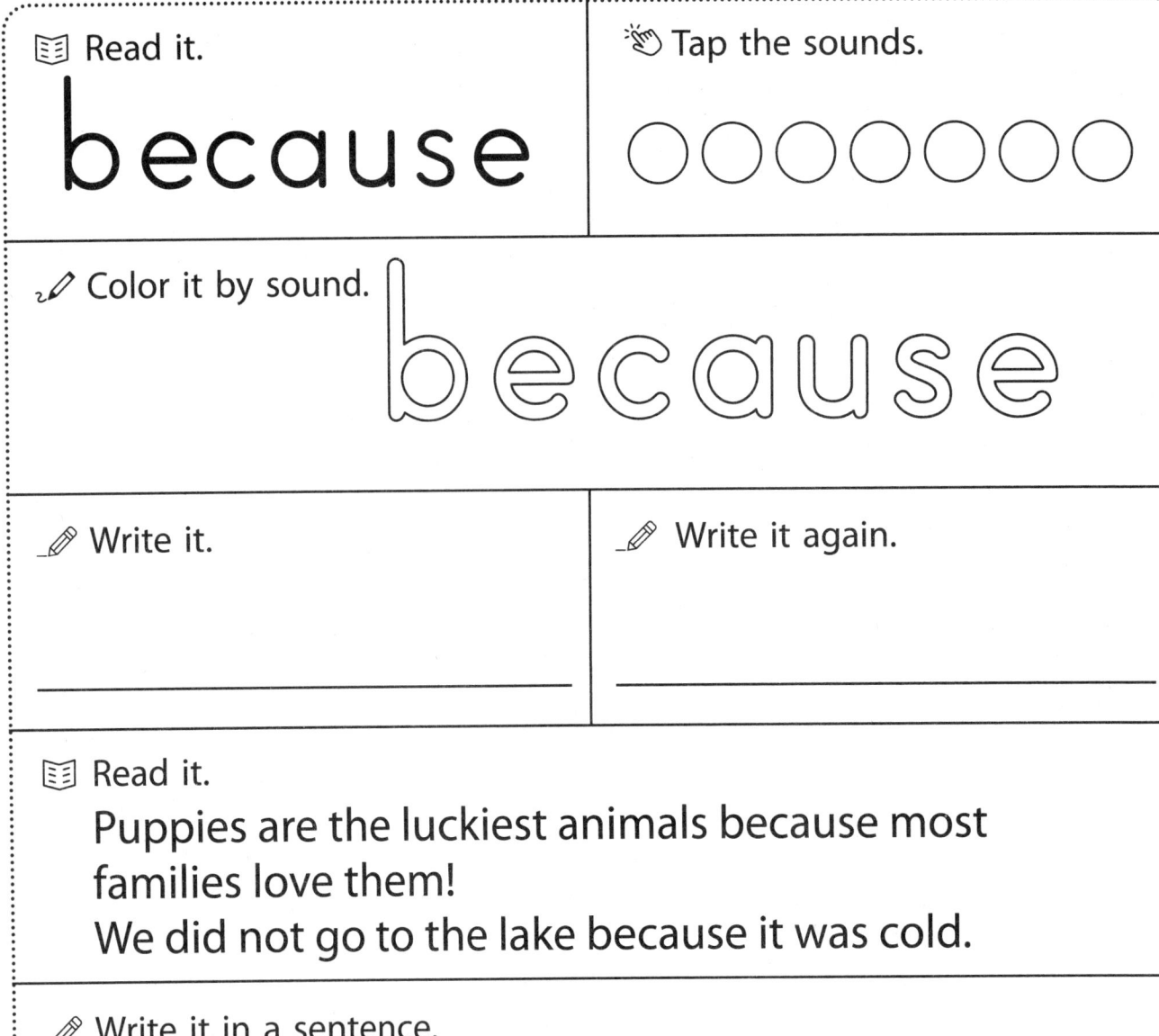

Read it.
Puppies are the luckiest animals because most families love them!
We did not go to the lake because it was cold.

Write it in a sentence.

Grade 2

Module 5 • Week 1

Name _____

Decodable Text

Boxes to Donate

Mom taped boxes and piled them up. Boxes and bags lined the hall.

The dog, Patches, nosed among them and whined.

"It is fine, Patches." Mom smiled. "We are not moving and ditching you. These are old things we've saved. We are donating them so others can get use out of them."

Patches nosed one of the boxes again, and Billy popped out of it, waving his hands.

"You got me," Billy said. "I was hiding to see if you could find me."

"Great timing," Mom said. "I was hoping you would be coming with me to help drop these things off. Then we can get some shaved ice from the ice stand."

"OK," Billy said. "I'm coming as long as we're taking Patches along for the ride!"

▶ Draw a picture that shows what you read in the text.

Name _____

Puppies

Dogs can have five or six puppies at a time. All puppies are cute, but some are fluffier, some are scruffier, and some are shaggier than others.

What do puppies like to do? Just like human babies, puppies like to take lots of naps! When they are not napping, puppies like to fetch balls, go on walks, and sniff for snacks. Puppies like tasks and are happier when they have a job to do.

Families can find puppies to adopt online. Or they can ask a vet where to go.

Puppies are the luckiest animals because most families love them!

▶ Draw a picture that shows what you read in the text.

Name _____

Vocabulary

Power Words: Match

Word Bank

| assured | contraption | exactly | intent |
| peered | precise | replica | respond |

▶ Write the Power Word from *Going Places* that best fits each item.

1. Which word could you use to describe an exact measurement? _____

2. Which word means the same as *promised*? _____

3. You may call a strange-looking object by this name. _____

4. Which word means something is a perfect copy of something else? _____

5. This word describes you when you won't give up on a task. _____

6. Which word means *looked at something closely*? _____

7. Which word is an adverb that means *in every way*? _____

8. This is what you do when someone asks a question. _____

Name _____

Suffixes -y, -ly

A **suffix** is a word part added to the end of a base word that changes the meaning of the word. The suffix –y means "having or being like something" and changes the base word to an **adjective**. The suffix –ly means "how" or "when" and changes the base word to an **adverb**.

Word Bank

bumpy   carefully   rocky

springy   weekly

▶ Complete each sentence with a word from the box. Circle *adjective* or *adverb* to tell what kind of word it is.

1. This path uphill is very _____ .   adjective   adverb

2. We must climb up _____ .   adjective   adverb

3. The moss feels _____ under my feet.   adjective   adverb

4. The rock feels very _____ .   adjective   adverb

5. We plan a new hike _____ .   adjective   adverb

▶ Add –y or –ly to each word and write the meaning for the new word.

6. fierce _____ means _____

7. itch _____ means _____

Name _____

Comprehension

Character

The **characters** in a story are the people or animals whom the story is about. We learn about characters by looking for clues about their traits. **External traits** tell how a character looks. **Internal traits** describe a character's personality.

▶ Answer the questions about *Going Places*.

🔍 Pages 89–91 What is Rafael doing on page 89? How does this help you get to know what he is like? How does Rafael feel in this part of the story and why? Why does he feel this way?

_____
_____
_____
_____
_____

🔍 Pages 92–94 What words would you use to describe Maya and why? How is Maya's perspective different from Rafael's?

_____
_____
_____
_____

Name _____

Vocabulary Strategy

Reference Sources

When you read, you may see a word that you do not know. Use a **dictionary** or a **glossary** to find out what the word means and how to pronounce it. Remember that the words in a dictionary or a glossary are listed in **alphabetical order**.

▶ Write the words in alphabetical order.

1. rough, munch, might
   _____

2. bellow, cool, bounced
   _____

▶ Pick two words used above to look up in a dictionary. Pronounce the words. Then write what the words mean.

3. _____
   _____

4. _____
   _____

Recount an Experience

When you **recount** an **experience**, you tell about something that happened to you. Stay on topic. Speak loudly and clearly in complete sentences. Tell about events in order. Share details and facts that will interest your listeners. Then be prepared to answer questions.

▶ Read one child's recounting of the race in *Going Places*. Then answer the questions.

An Amazing Race

We were all waiting for the race to begin. There were more than a dozen go-carts. Each one looked the same.

Then Maya and Rafael arrived with their go-cart. People pointed and laughed. Their go-cart looked like a plane! It had wings and a propeller! I was really confused.

Once I went on a plane to Chicago. Anyway, the race started, and of course the plane won. Everyone cheered, and I jumped up and down. Before the plane won, it swooped in the air!

Name _____

Speaking and Listening

1. What is the topic of the story?

_____

_____

2. What details does the speaker give about Maya's go-cart?

_____

_____

3. Which sentence in the recounting is not about the topic?

_____

_____

4. Which sentence in the recounting is out of order?

_____

_____

5. What are two questions you might ask the speaker?

_____

_____

_____

Name _____

Consonant + *le*

Consonant + *le* is a type of final stable syllable. In this syllable, the consonant stands for its own sound, the *l* stands for /l/, and the *e* is always silent. The word *candle* has a consonant + *le* syllable.

▶ Choose and write the word that names the picture. Circle the consonant + *le* syllable.

bicycle fiddle simple	**baffles uncle bubbles**
 _____	 _____
kettle sample fumble	**goggle giggle table**
 _____	 _____
cuddle candle crinkle	**ripple rumble rattle**
 _____	 _____

Phonics

Grade 2   131   Module 5 • Week 2

Consonant + le

Consonant + *le* is a type of final stable syllable. In this syllable, the consonant stands for its own sound, the *l* stands for /l/, and the *e* is always silent. The word *candle* has a consonant + *le* syllable.

▶ Choose and write two words to complete each sentence.

1. My _____ gave me a _____ to munch on while we drove home.

   twinkle   **pickle**   **hobble**   **uncle**

2. We must be _____ when we pet the _____ baby chick.

   little   **gentle**   **tickle**   **bubble**

3. The flame of the _____ began to _____ in the wind.

   ramble   **cuddle**   **candle**   **wobble**

4. I held the hot _____ by the _____ and set it on the table.

   kettle   **snuggle**   **handle**   **buckle**

5. The funny _____ made me _____ so much!

   tumble   **giggle**   **puzzle**   **riddle**

6. I had to quickly _____ up the _____ gym at recess.

   scramble   **single**   **fiddle**   **jungle**

Name _____

Irregular Words

Read and Spell

Read and spell this word to be a better reader.

📖 Read it.

other

👆 Tap the sounds.

○ ○ ○ ○ ○ ○ ○

✏️ Color it by sound.

other

✏️ Write it.

_____

✏️ Write it again.

_____

📖 Read it.

I will take two and give my uncle the other.

I like the other puzzle best.

✏️ Write it in a sentence.

_____

_____

Grade 2   133   Module 5 • Week 2

Name _____

Irregular Words

Read and Spell

Read and spell this word to be a better reader.

📖 Read it.

another

👆 Tap the sounds.

○ ○ ○ ○ ○ ○ ○

✏️ Color it by sound.

another

✏️ Write it.

_____

✏️ Write it again.

_____

📖 Read it.

She also has another ring that makes bubbles with funny shapes.
Can we get another candle?

✏️ Write it in a sentence.

_____

_____

Name _____

Decodable Text

The Fun Fest

Today is the Fun Fest at Maple Lake Camp. Axle, Darby, and Madge do acts for all the kids.

Madge stacks blocks and logs on a table. She stands on top of the pile and it wobbles, but it does not topple!

Axle and Darby tell jokes and riddles that make the kids chuckle and giggle.

Then they all flip and tumble on mats. One of them lifts two others. They are stacked up tall but do not stumble!

Last, Darby does a bubble act. She puts a huge tub on the stage and drizzles bubble mix into it. Then she dips a big ring in the tub and wiggles it up. The bubble is as tall as she is! She also has another ring that makes bubbles with funny shapes.

At the end, the kids clap and chant for all the acts.

▶ Draw a picture that shows what you read in the text.

Name _____

Apple Picking

"Are you all set for apple picking?" Gran asked.

"I am!" I said as I held up a big mesh bag with handles. "I can fit a lot of apples in this sack."

Gran gave me some tips about picking apples. "Be gentle when you go in for an apple. If the branches jiggle a lot, apples can fall and smash."

But I was gentle, so the branches did not wobble.

Then Gran helped me use a grabbing stick so I could pick a huge apple that was at the top of a branch.

"When can we sample the apples?" I asked.

"Once we wash them," Gran said. "Then we can gobble them up!"

▶ Draw a picture that shows what you read in the text.

Name _____

Vocabulary

Power Words: Yes or No?

Word Bank

honored   success   rare   relay

▶ Read each sentence. Circle **YES** if the word makes sense or **NO** if it does not. Rewrite the sentence so it makes sense.

1. Baseball is a **rare** sport in America.

   YES   NO

   _____

   _____

2. Runners on a **relay** team must run fast for the team to have **success**.

   YES   NO

   _____

   _____

3. A famous person may be **honored** with a statue.

   YES   NO

   _____

   _____

Name _____

Comprehension

Text Features

Authors may use different text features to organize information. This makes the information easier for the reader to find. **Captions** are words or sentences about photos. **Headings** are titles for a page or section of text. **Fact boxes** give extra information about a topic.

▶ Answer the questions about *Wilma Rudolph: Against All Odds*.

🔍 Pages 108–110 What information do the headings give you? Do you think "Little Wilma" is a good heading for page 108? Explain.

_____

_____

_____

_____

🔍 Pages 112–113 What do you learn from these captions? What information do you learn in the fact box? Why didn't the author put this information in the main text?

_____

_____

_____

_____

_____

Name _____

Phonics Review

Consonant + *le* is a type of final stable syllable. In this syllable, the consonant stands for its own sound, the *l* stands for /l/, and the *e* is always silent. The word *candle* has a consonant + *le* syllable.

▶ Choose and write a word to complete each sentence.

1. I am having lunch with my _____ and his wife.

   uncle   noble   bubble

2. I am going to make _____ cakes with a maple drizzle.

   single   scribble   apple

3. I set the plate of cakes in the middle of the _____ .

   simple   table   cable

4. Then I set the _____ on the stove to get it hot.

   tickle   cuddle   kettle

5. I lit a _____ to make my home smell nice.

   candle   pickle   bubble

6. I hope my uncle likes the _____ lunch I made!

   jiggle   cable   simple

Name _____

Generative Vocabulary

Prefix dis-

The **prefix** *dis–* means "not" or "opposite." You can use the meaning of the prefix and the **base word** to figure out the meaning of a new word. When you are not sure about the meaning of a base word, you can use a dictionary.

Word Bank

disappear   disbelieve   disconnect

▶ Complete each sentence using a word from the box. If you are unsure about the meaning of a word, you can look it up in the dictionary.

1. If you _____ the telephone, you will not receive the call.

2. It is easy to _____ that you flew to the moon last night!

3. Jasmine likes to watch the deer _____ into the woods.

▶ Add the word part *dis–* to each word. Then write a sentence using the new word. If you are not sure of the base word's meaning, check a dictionary.

4. please: _____

5. place: _____

Name _____

Vocabulary

Power Words: Draw and Write

Word Bank

advice   earned   equal   politics

▶ Draw a picture or write words that will help you remember each Power Word from *Great Leaders*. Try to write more than you draw.

1. advice

2. earned

3. equal

4. politics

Name _____

Comprehension

Ideas and Support

When authors write to **persuade**, they want readers to agree with them or to do something. First, an author states an **opinion** that tells what they think or believe. Then they give **reasons** to support the opinion. Strong reasons include **facts**, or things that can be proved. That helps persuade the reader to agree with the author.

▶ Answer the questions about *Great Leaders*.

🔍 Pages 122–125 What does Olivia think of Abigail Adams? Is this a fact or an opinion? Explain. How do the examples about what Abigail did for women's rights help Olivia persuade readers?

_____

_____

_____

_____

🔍 Pages 126–130 What belief does Anthony share with readers? Is this a fact or an opinion? What does Anthony want readers to do?

_____

_____

_____

Name _____

Vowel Teams ee, ea, ey

A vowel team is a combination of letters that represent a single vowel sound.

The vowel team *ee* stands for the long e sound, /ē/.

The vowel team *ea* can also stand for the long e sound.

The vowel team *ey* can also stand for the long e sound.

▶ Write the word that names the picture. Circle the grapheme that stands for the long e sound.

bees   donkey   beads

_____

treat   teeth   three

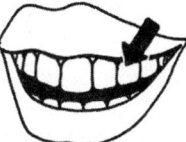

_____

leaf   key   creek

_____

sheep   donkey   seal

_____

needle   eagle   chimney

_____

green   tree   feast

_____

Name _____

Vowel Teams ee, ea, ey

Phonics

You can spell long *e* with *ee*, as in *sheep*; *ea*, as in *leaf*; or *ey*, as in *key*.

▶ Read each word. Write the word or words that rhyme with it.

Word Bank

free
teach
teeth
donkey
each
wheel
team
speak
sneeze
sheep
mean
weave

1. reach   _____   _____
2. leave   _____   _____
3. peel   _____   _____
4. sneak   _____   _____
5. dream   _____   _____
6. see   _____   _____
7. peep   _____   _____
8. clean   _____   _____
9. freeze _____   _____
10. key   _____   _____

▶ Which word did you not use? Write a sentence for it.

_____
_____
_____

Name _____

Irregular Words

Read and Spell

Read and spell this word to be a better reader.

📖 Read it.

always

👆 Tap the sounds.

○ ○ ○ ○ ○ ○ ○

✏️ Color it by sound.

always

✏️ Write it.

_____

✏️ Write it again.

_____

📖 Read it.

But a seal can always beat you in a race!

The trees always seem tiny at this stage.

✏️ Write it in a sentence.

_____

_____

Grade 2 — 143 — Module 5 • Week 3

Irregular Words

Name _____

Read and Spell

Read and spell this word to be a better reader.

📖 Read it.

almost

👆 Tap the sounds.

○ ○ ○ ○ ○ ○ ○

✏️ Color it by sound.

almost

✏️ Write it.

_____

✏️ Write it again.

_____

📖 Read it.

When they do sleep, they can bob almost like they are standing in the sea.
I almost did not make it to the meeting!

✏️ Write it in a sentence.

_____

_____

Grade 2   143a   Module 5 • Week 3

Name _____

Decodable Text

Seals

Did you know that seals spend time in the sea and on land?

In the sea, seals dive deep to catch fish for a meal. A seal's strong teeth help it grab a fish. To rest from swimming, seals sit on sheets of ice. They do not freeze, because they have thick bits of fat on them.

Seals do not need a lot of sleep. When they do sleep, they can bob almost like they are standing in the sea.

Seals do not need to be wet all of the time. Some seals can be on a beach for a week. Seals do not have feet, so they roll and hobble in the sand. But a seal can always beat you in a race!

▶ Draw a picture that shows what you read in the text.

Name _____

Decodable Text

Planting Trees

The Green Team is a club that does things to help the planet. We pick up trash from sidewalks, grass, and beaches. We teach other kids key tips to reduce waste. And we plant trees.

Today, we are planting three maple trees in a sunny spot of land.

The trees always seem tiny at this stage, but in time, they will get bigger and taller.

To plant the trees, we dig three deep holes. Then we ease each tree into one of the holes. We hold the tree in place, fill in the hole, and then get the base wet.

We will help each tree meet its needs so it can live to be an adult tree. Then other kids can relax in the shade of its branches.

▶ Draw a picture that shows what you read in the text.

Name _____

Vocabulary

Power Words: Match

Word Bank

capital	charge	council	laws
members	state	solve	troop

▶ Write the Power Word from *Who Are Government's Leaders?* that best fits each item.

1. Which word names a place with many towns and cities? _____

2. This is a word that names a group of people in a club. _____

3. These are rules that keep people safe. _____

4. Which word names the action of someone who leads a group? _____

5. Which word names a group of people who are leaders? _____

6. This is where leaders of a government meet. _____

7. These are people who belong to a group. _____

8. A clue will help a detective do this to a problem. _____

Name _____

Content-Area Words

Some informational texts have special words about a social studies or science topic. Readers may use **context clues** to figure out the meaning of these **content-area words**. Context clues are the words and sentences around an unfamiliar word that can be clues to its meaning.

▶ Answer the questions about *Who Are Government's Leaders?*

🔍 Page 138 Which sentence on this page helps you define *governor*? Why was this sentence more helpful than the one before it? How else could you find the meaning of this word?

_____

_____

_____

_____

🔍 Page 139 Does what you know about the word *citizens* fit the way the word is used here? Explain.

_____

_____

_____

Name _____

Phonics

Vowel Teams ee, ea, ey

A vowel team is a combination of letters that represent a single vowel sound.

The vowel team *ee* stands for the long *e* sound, /ē/.
The vowel team *ea* can also stand for the long *e* sound.
The vowel team *ey* can also stand for the long *e* sound.

▶ Read each sentence. Then choose the correct word to complete the sentence and write it in the blank.

1. I watched a leaf fall off the _____ .

   treat   tree   trip

2. I used the _____ to open the locked box.

   keep   kelp   key

3. I try to keep my _____ nice and white.

   tin   teeth   this

4. It is kind to say _____ when asking for something.

   please   peas   peace

5. I like to eat green beans and _____ !

   meat   neat   met

Name _____

Words That Name People

Nouns are words that name people, places, or things. Nouns that name people tell who they are, what they do, or give a title. If you do not know what a noun means, you can look it up in a dictionary.

▶ Draw a picture for each noun. If you are unsure about the noun, you can look it up in a dictionary.

1. baker	2. firefighter

Word Bank

baby   grandfather   pilot   queen

▶ Write the noun from the box that best completes each sentence. If you are not sure of a word's meaning, check the dictionary.

3. I visit my _____ every Sunday.

4. The _____ is the leader of her country.

5. The _____ will fly the airplane.

6. The cute _____ crawled toward the toy.

Phonics

Name _____

Vowel Teams ai, ay

A vowel team is a combination of letters that represent a single vowel sound.

The vowel team *ai* stands for the long *a* sound /ā/.

The vowel team *ay* also stands for the long *a* sound /ā/.

▶ Write two words to complete each sentence.

1. We have to _____ inside since it is going to _____ today.

    main   made   rain   stay

2. They have to wait in the _____ for the _____ to come.

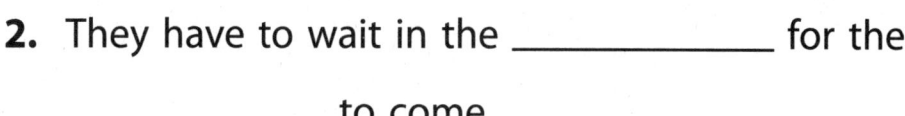

    spray   train   take   subway

3. My pet _____ is _____ with white dots.

    paid   play   gray   snail

4. She _____ for the _____ of snacks with cash.

    stay   clay   tray   paid

5. "It is going to be a sunny _____ !" Gail _____ .

    day   laid   relay   exclaims

Name _____

Phonics

Vowel Teams ey, eigh

A vowel team is a combination of letters that represent a single vowel sound.
The vowel team *ey* can stand for the long *a* sound, /ā/.
The vowel team *eigh* can also stand for the long *a* sound, /ā/.

▶ Write the word from the word bank that best completes each sentence.

Word Bank

eight
they
weight
obey
hey
sleigh
prey
weigh
eighteen
neigh

1. Did _____ take the train into the city?

2. It is fun to ride in a _____ when it is cold.

3. When I am _____, I will be able to vote.

4. What can we use to find the _____ of things?

5. The colt gave a big _____ as it ran in the grass.

6. Some snakes _____ on mice and rats, and some eat frogs and fish.

7. I have to teach my pet to _____ when it is on a leash.

Phonics

Name _____

Vowel Teams *ai, ay, ey, eigh*

A vowel team is a combination of letters that represent a single vowel sound.

The vowel team *ai* stands for the long *a* sound /ā/.
The vowel team *ay* also stands for the long *a* sound /ā/.
The vowel team *ey* can stand for the long *a* sound, /ā/.
The vowel team *eigh* can also stand for the long *a* sound, /ā/.

▶ Read the clues. Write the word that answers the clue.

1. We do this with games, balls, and pals. _____

    sleigh   chain   play

2. I take things long ways on my rails. _____

    train   prey   stray

3. I name a pile of dry grasses. _____

    driveway   eighteen   haystack

4. My links connect things. _____

    weigh   chain   stray

5. I name a thing you can eat. _____

    raisin   obey   spray

Name _____

Set Sail at Sunset

Do you need a way to relax at the end of a long week? Then I know just the thing for you to do!

Come for a sunset sail on the bay with Shay's Sailing Team. Shay and his team have been sailing for two decades, so you can feel safe with them!

Shay's Sailing Team provides trips mainly for sunrise, sunset, or the full day. Log onto the team's website. Then pick and pay for the day, time, and trip length that you want. You should also pick a rain date in case it rains on the day of your planned trip.

As you sail, you can relax and take in all that is around you. Or, you can ask the team to teach you about sailing. They may even let you try your hand at the wheel!

▶ Draw a picture that shows what you read in the text.

Name _____

Decodable Text

Eagles

What is that gliding in the sky? It is an eagle!

From tip to tip, an eagle's wings can reach almost eight feet. And an eagle's weight is about the same as a cat's.

Eagles can make long trips and fly to the tops of tall trees. That is where they make nests.

An eagle can use sticks and twigs to make a big nest. Eagles tend to use the same home again and again.

Eagles can see well, which helps them hunt for prey. They can see small animals, such as rabbits, up to three miles away! Eagles prey on fish as well. An eagle's fixed grip comes in handy to hold fish while flying. From time to time, eagles even steal prey from other animals.

▶ Draw a picture that shows what you read in the text.

Name _____

Vocabulary

Power Words: Match

Word Bank

| clings | damage | excess | funnel |
| occur | pellets | predict | tough |

▶ Write the Power Word from *Wild Weather* that best fits each item.

1. Which word means the opposite of *easy*? _____

2. This word means I have too much of something. _____

3. Which word names tiny balls of something? _____

4. If you do this, you say what you think will happen in the future. _____

5. Which word means the opposite of *fix*? _____

6. Which word means *to take place*? _____

7. Which word could be a cloud's shape? _____

8. This word means the same as *sticks to*. _____

Generative Vocabulary

Name _____

Suffixes –er, –est

Add –er to the end of an **adjective**, or describing word, to compare two things. Add –est to compare three or more things.

▶ Read the word and look at the pictures. Add –er or –est to the end of the base word. Then write a sentence about the pictures using the new word.

1.

big: _____ : _____

_____

2.

heavy: _____ : _____

_____

▶ Add –er and –est to the base word *easy*. On the lines below, write a sentence using each of the new words.

3. _____ : _____

_____

4. _____ : _____

_____

Grade 2 · 155 · Module 6 • Week 1

Name _____

Comprehension

Text Organization

Text organization is the way an author shares information in a text so readers will understand it. Texts organized by **cause** and **effect** describe how one event leads to another event. A cause is something that happens. An effect is what happens because of the cause.

▶ Answer the questions about *Wild Weather*.

🔍 Pages 160–161 What do you notice about the way the author organizes the text on these pages? What causes warm air to rise? What is the effect?

_____

_____

_____

_____

🔍 Pages 168–169 What type of wild weather is Sonny asking about? What does Chuck say is the cause of snowflakes forming? What is the effect of the ground being cold? Why do you think the author organizes the text this way?

_____

_____

_____

_____

Name _____

Vocabulary Strategy

Homophones

Homophones sound alike but do not have the same spelling or meanings. Look for **context clues** and the word's spelling to figure out its meaning. You can also use a dictionary.

Word Bank

hole   sea   see   whole

▶ Choose a homophone to complete each sentence. Write its meaning on the line.

1. The squirrel dug a _____ to hide a nut.
_____

2. Dad wears glasses to help him _____ what he is reading.
_____

3. Jackson likes to sit on the beach and look at the _____ .
_____

4. Our _____ class will sing a song together at the assembly.
_____

▶ Find each word in a dictionary. Then write a sentence.

5. break: _____

6. brake: _____

Media Literacy

Name _____

Digital Tools and Texts

A **digital tool** is a type of technology, like a computer, tablet, or smartphone. A **digital text** is a text you read or experience using digital tools. A **presentation** is a formal way to share information with others. You can use a presentation tool, like a digital slide, when presenting.

▶ Read the digital text below. Then answer questions about it.

Wild Weather Facts: Tornadoes!

Tornadoes form when strong winds spin in a circle.
A tornado is a large gray cloud that is wide at the top and skinny at the bottom.

Most tornadoes only last a few minutes, but some are very strong.

Take cover if you see one!

For more information about wild weather, click on the **Wild Weather Facts** homepage.

TORNADO VIDEOS

TORNADO SOUNDS

TORNADO SAFETY TIPS

1. What is a digital tool that you could use to find and read this digital text?

_____

Name _____

Media Literacy

2. Circle the letters of the special features you see in "Wild Weather Facts: Tornadoes!"

   a. Video recording

   b. Hyperlink

   c. Interactive diagram

   d. Audio recording

3. Which special feature would you click on to find information about other kinds of wild weather?

   _____

   _____

   _____

▶ Share a fact you learned about tornadoes. Write and draw in the box to make a slide you could use to present the information.

Phonics

Name _____

Vowel Teams ow, oa, oe

A vowel team is a combination of letters that represent a single vowel sound.

The vowel team *ow* can stand for the long *o* sound, /ō/.

The vowel team *oa* also stands for the long *o* sound.

The vowel team *oe* also stands for the long *o* sound.

▶ Choose and write two words to complete each sentence.

1. Joan went on a _____ stroll along the _____ .

    slow   toe   coast   doe

2. She watched the sails of the _____ _____ in the wind.

    snow   blow   boats   woe

3. A _____ _____ on the sandy beach.

    crowed   toast   croaked   toad

4. She dipped her _____ in the cold sea _____ .

    toe   goat   coach   foam

5. Then Joan went for a _____ in the _____ sea.

    shallow   doe   soak   bowl

Grade 2   160   Module 6 • Week 2
© Houghton Mifflin Harcourt Publishing Company. All rights reserved.

Name _____

Phonics

Vowel Teams ow, oa, oe

The vowel teams *ow, oa,* and *oe* can all stand for the long *o* sound, /ō/.

▶ Read each incomplete sentence. Write the word from the word bank that best completes each sentence.

Spelling Words

own
soap
float
doe
toe
goals
goat
flow
loaf
throw
roast

1. Mom made _____ beef. _____

2. Use _____ to wash the dishes. _____

3. Who made the most _____? _____

4. _____ the ball to me. _____

5. We can milk a _____. _____

6. The _____ jumped across the grass. _____

7. I can _____ on my back. _____

8. I _____ that pen. _____

9. I stubbed my _____ on the wall. _____

▶ Write a sentence for each of the words in the word bank you did not use.

_____

_____

_____

Name _____

Irregular Words

Read and Spell

Read and spell this word to be a better reader.

📖 Read it.

both

👆 Tap the sounds.

◯ ◯ ◯ ◯ ◯ ◯ ◯

✏️ Color it by sound.

both

✏️ Write it.

_____

✏️ Write it again.

_____

📖 Read it.

Both boats sail away.

I like to eat both oats and sweets.

✏️ Write it in a sentence.

_____

_____

Grade 2 162 Module 6 • Week 2
© Houghton Mifflin Harcourt Publishing Company. All rights reserved.

Name _____

Irregular Words

Read and Spell

Read and spell this word to be a better reader.

📖 Read it.

only

👆 Tap the sounds.

○ ○ ○ ○ ○ ○ ○

✏️ Color it by sound.

only

✏️ Write it.

_____

✏️ Write it again.

_____

📖 Read it.

Only when the winds slow, do I put on my coat and dash out.
This is the only time I have seen snow!

✏️ Write it in a sentence.

_____

_____

Grade 2   162a   Module 6 • Week 2

Name _____

Decodable Text

Snow Day

I watch as big, twinkling snowflakes float from the sky.

"Mom, when can I play in the snow?" I ask.

"When you eat your oats and toast." Mom peeks outside. "And when the wind doesn't blow so much."

Only when the winds slow, do I put on my coat and dash out. Joe is there!

"I want to make a snowman," Joe tells me.

"I want to make a snow boat," I say.

"We can put a snowman in a snow boat!" Joe says.

"Then he can row in the snow," I add.

We play till the sun is low and our toes are cold. Then Joe goes home and I go inside.

▶ Draw a picture that shows what you read in the text.

Name _____

Decodable Text

Boats on the Coast

There are a lot of boats along the coast. Some boats are big, and some are small. Some boats need gas to go, and others use wind.

Some kids sail in two sailboats. These boats need wind to go. There is a strong wind in the bay. The kids put the sails up. Both boats sail away.

A tugboat tows a big boat loaded with freight. The freight in this boat includes bushels of grain.

At the dock, a little rowboat floats. A woman gets in the little boat and rows to the cove, where she teaches kids to row.

▶ Draw a picture that shows what you read in the text.

Name _____

Vocabulary

Power Words: Draw and Write

Word Bank

advantages   average   front   impressed

▶ Draw a picture or write words that will help you remember each Power Word from *Cloudette*. Try to write more than you draw.

1. advantages

2. average

3. front

4. impressed

Name _____

Comprehension

Point of View

Point of view describes the way readers see things happen in a story. If a story is told from first-person point of view, a character in the story is the narrator. A story told from third-person point of view has an outside narrator.

▶ Answer the questions about *Cloudette*.

🔍 Pages 182–183 Is this story written in first-person or third-person point of view? How do you know?

_____
_____
_____
_____

🔍 Pages 186–187 What does the narrator tell about Cloudette? How would the words change if the story were told in first-person point of view?

_____
_____
_____
_____

Name _____

Phonics

Phonics Review

A vowel team is a combination of letters that represent a single vowel sound.

The vowel team *ow* can stand for the long *o* sound, /ō/.

The vowel team *oa* also stands for the long *o* sound.

The vowel team *oe* also stands for the long *o* sound.

▶ Choose and write the word that answers each riddle.

1. A lemon, a banana, and the sun are all this shade.

_____

    hoe   yellow   bowl   soak

2. A boat does this on the sea. _____

    float   soak   grow   hollow

3. This is a place a pet fish lives. _____

    toe   grow   groan   bowl

4. This can fall from the sky when it is cold. _____

    snow   boat   grow   doe

5. Feet can have ten of these. _____

    cloak   toes   shadow   throw

Prefixes un-, re-

The **prefix** un– means "to reverse" or "not." The prefix re– means "again." Use the meaning of the prefix and the **base word** to figure out the meaning of the new word. If you are not sure about the meaning of a base word, you can use a dictionary.

▶ Add un– or re– to each base word below to make a new word. Then draw a line to match the word to its definition.

1. ____happy   not healthy

2. ____healthy   to appear again

3. ____appear   to pay again

4. ____pay   not happy

▶ Circle the word that completes the sentence. Check a dictionary if you are unsure about the meaning of a word.

5. I was bored during the movie because the story was _____ .

   interesting   uninteresting

6. I will _____ the beans, even though I did not like them the first time.

   retry   try

7. A story that is fiction is usually _____ .

   untrue   true

Name _____

Vocabulary

Power Words: Yes or No?

Word Bank

flash gusts layer supplies

▶ Read each sentence. Circle **YES** if the word makes sense or **NO** if it does not. Rewrite the sentence so it makes sense.

1. An extra **layer** of clothing will keep you warm.

   YES   NO

   _____

2. Bottles of water are good **supplies** to have during a storm.

   YES   NO

   _____

3. A **flash** of light is not bright.

   YES   NO

   _____

4. You are more likely to feel **gusts** indoors.

   YES   NO

   _____

Name _____

Comprehension

Text Features

Authors of informational texts often use different kinds of text features to explain ideas or to help readers find information. A **caption** is words or sentences that describe a picture. A **heading** is the title of a page or section of a text. A **fact box** is a feature with extra information about the topic.

▶ Answer the questions about *Get Ready for Weather*.

🔍 Page 207 How does the caption tell more about the picture? What do the different symbols in the chart stand for?

_____
_____
_____
_____

🔍 Pages 208–209 What does the heading tell you about the information you will read in this part of the text? Why did the author put some information about lightning in the Try This! box?

_____
_____
_____
_____

Phonics

Name _____

Vowel Teams *ie, igh*

A vowel team is a combination of letters that represent a single vowel sound.
The vowel team *ie* stands for the long *i* sound, /ī/.
The vowel team *igh* can also stand for the long *i* sound.

▶ Choose and write the word that completes each sentence.

1. The lamp needs a _____ bulb.

   lie   line   light

2. I have to _____ the bow to get my cleat on.

   tightly   untie   retile

3. I helped my dad bake the _____ for the bake sale.

   right   light   pie

4. I hung the pants on the line in the _____ sun to dry.

   bright   lie   tie

5. I held the trophy up _____ after I won the race!

   sight   high   tight

Name _____

Phonics

Vowel Teams *ie, igh*

The vowel team *ie* stands for the long *i* sound. The vowel team *igh* can also stand for the long *i* sound.

▶ Read each clue. Write the word from the word bank that answers each clue on the line.

Word Bank
night
tie
bright
pie
sigh
lie
right
high
light
tight

1. We slice this to eat it _____

2. Breathe out slowly _____

3. Not left _____

4. What we do with laces _____

5. Not low _____

6. Not day _____

7. The sun gives us this _____

8. A snug fit _____

▶ Write a sentence for each of the words in the word bank you did not use.

_____

_____

_____

Irregular Words

Name _____

Read and Spell

Read and spell this word to be a better reader.

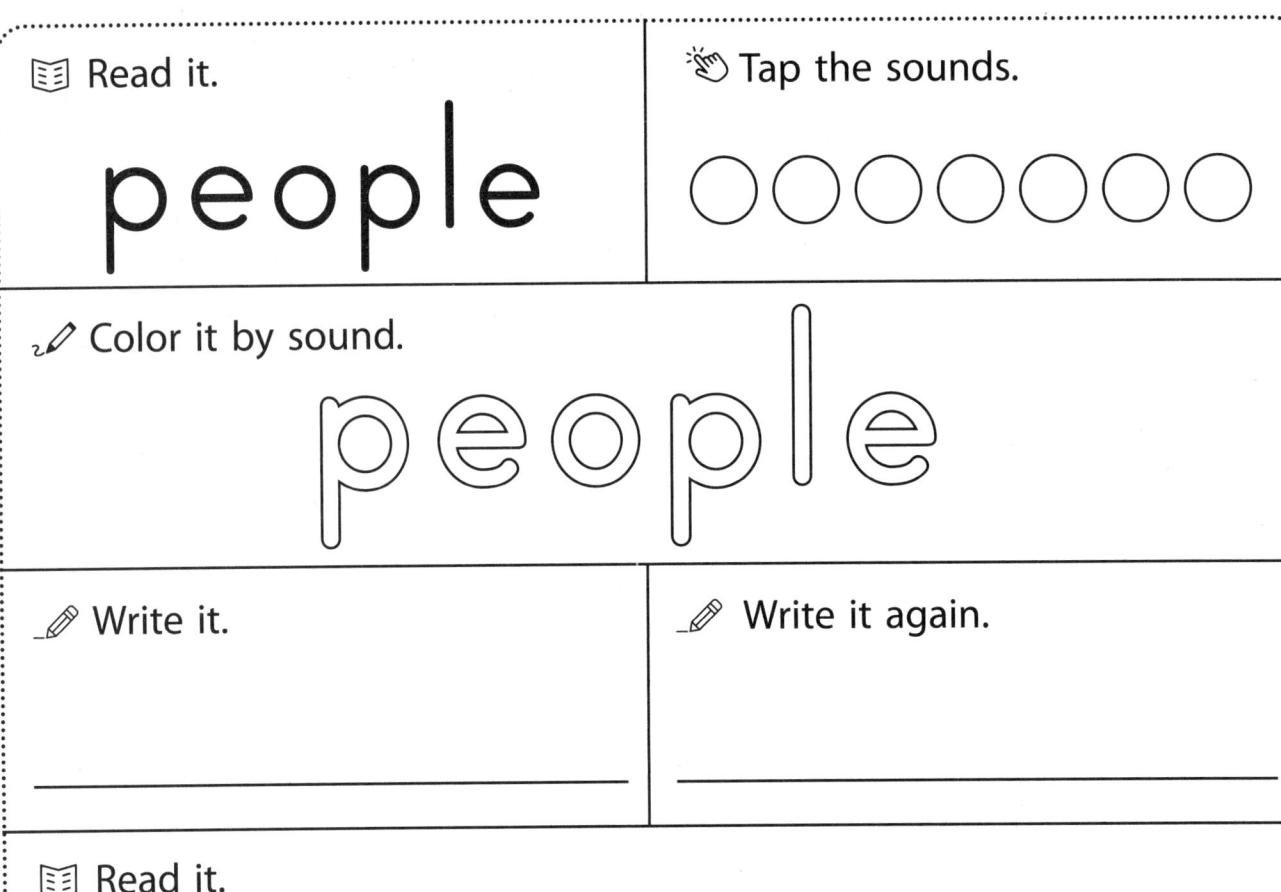

📖 Read it.

The people stretched the picnic blanket across the grass.
All of the people clapped when the band finished!

✏️ Write it in a sentence.

_____

_____

Name _____

Decodable Text

A Thump in the Night

Thump! I woke up with a jolt.

I'm not going to lie. It gave me a bit of a fright, but it was late at night, and I didn't want to wake Mom and Dad.

I slipped out of bed and walked to my closet, but I couldn't see anything. I tapped the light switch on the wall, and then I could see what made the thump.

"Pickles!" I cried. "You gave me a fright!"

My baseball mitt was on my desk, and my cat, Pickles, was nuzzled inside of it. My baseball had dropped to the floor.

Pickles stayed right where she was and blinked at me.

"You're lucky you are cute," I sighed. I picked up the ball, put it on a shelf, and got into my bed.

"Night, Pickles," I said as I drifted back to sleep.

▶ Draw a picture that shows what you read in the text.

Name _____

Decodable Text

The Picnic

The people stretched the picnic blanket across the grass and put a rock on each edge to hold it in place. The sun was bright, and beams of light shone on the blanket.

"It feels nice to sit in the sun," Dwight said, opening the picnic basket.

He set out fried chicken and peaches, Mandy put out cold drinks, and Sloane set out an apple pie. It all smelled great!

They ate the chicken and peaches. Then Dwight asked, "Is it time for pie?"

"Yes!" Sloane said. "I will cut it into slices. Can you pass the plates, Mandy?"

"Sit tight," Mandy said as she dug in the basket. "I tried to find them, but I can't. We must not have brought them."

Dwight checked his backpack, but he couldn't find them.

"No problem!" Mandy said. "We can put the pie on napkins. It will taste the same."

▶ Draw a picture that shows what you read in the text.

Name _____

Vocabulary

Power Words: Match

Word Bank

| covers | creep | glide | rumble |
| shimmering | slather | slithering | splatter |

▶ Write the Power Word from *Whatever the Weather* that best fits each item.

1. This is a word that means *goes over*. _____

2. This is the sound of thunder. _____

3. Your teacher might use this word to tell you to use a lot of glue. _____

4. Which word describes how something is shining? _____

5. If you see a snake in the grass, it is moving like this. _____

6. Which word can mean the opposite of *run past*? _____

7. This is how drops of a liquid fall. _____

8. Which word describes a smooth and easy movement? _____

Name _____

Elements of Poetry

Poetry is a special kind of writing. Poems have **rhythm, patterns,** and **stanzas.** Some poems **rhyme** or have repetition. Poems also have **descriptive** and **figurative language** to help readers picture what the poet sees in his or her mind.

▶ Answer the questions about *Whatever the Weather*.

🔍 Pages 220–221 What words or phrases does the poet use to help you imagine what the rain sounds like? How do the spaces between the words help create rhythm?

_____

_____

_____

_____

🔍 Page 224 Why did the poet repeat some of the lines in this poem? How does that repetition help you understand the poem's important ideas?

_____

_____

_____

_____

Phonics Review

A vowel team is a combination of letters that represent a single vowel sound.
The vowel team *ie* stands for the long *i* sound, /ī/.
The vowel team *igh* can also stand for the long *i* sound.

▶ Choose and write the word that completes each sentence.

1. Tonight, I am helping Dad make a _____ .

   sight   pie   light

2. It takes all my _____ to roll the thick crust!

   die   tight   might

3. Dad grabs the spice off the _____ shelf.

   high   light   tie

4. We fill the pie, then pinch the edges _____ .

   lie   tight   fright

5. I brush the pie with a _____ coat of egg wash.

   light   bright   die

6. We think the pie is going to taste just _____!

   sigh   fight   right

Name _____

Inflections –ed, –ing

Add *–ed* to the end of a **verb** to tell about an action in the past. Add *–ing* to the end of a verb to tell about an action that is happening in the present or that may happen in the future.

▶ Add *–ed* or *–ing* to the word in parentheses to complete the sentences. Write the word on the line. Remember, there may be spelling changes to the verb when you add the ending.

1. (walk) He _____ to school in the rain yesterday.

2. (listen) I will be _____ to the weather report tomorrow.

3. (hope) Emma is _____ for a sunny day today.

4. (pile) The snow _____ up on the sidewalk yesterday.

5. (happen) Another storm will be _____ this week.

▶ Choose one verb about weather: *rain, sleet, snow, melt, flood*. Write a sentence using each form of the verb.

6. past: _____

7. present: _____

8. future: _____

VC/CV Syllable Division Pattern

When a word has two consonants between two vowels, the Rabbit Rule tells us to divide between the consonants (rab-bit).

▶ Draw a line (/) to divide each word into syllables.

insects	ribbon	problem
cactus	submit	picnic

▶ Use the words above to complete the sentences.

1. Greg got each math _____ right.

2. Flies, bees, and beetles are all kinds of _____ .

3. I have a _____ plant by my window so it can get sun.

4. I used my laptop to _____ my essay.

5. Mom tied a _____ on the gift.

6. It is a beautiful day to have a _____ .

Name _____

Phonics

VC/CV Syllable Division Pattern

When a word has two consonants between two vowels, the Rabbit Rule tells us to divide between the consonants (*rab-bit*).

▶ Look at each picture. Write the word from the word bank that matches the picture. Then break apart the word into two chunks.

Word Bank

picnic   raincoat   basket   napkin   magnet

1. _____

2. _____

3. _____

4. _____

5. _____

Grade 2   179   Module 7 • Week 1
© Houghton Mifflin Harcourt Publishing Company. All rights reserved.

Name _____

Phonics Review

When a word has two consonants between two vowels, the Rabbit Rule tells us to divide between between the consonants (*rab-bit*).

▶ Draw a line (/) to divide each word into syllables.

rabbit	fabric	object
penny	splendid	meatloaf

▶ Use the words above to complete the sentences.

1. My grandma makes the best _____ with green beans.

2. I cut the _____ into strips and then stitched them into a quilt.

3. The _____ ran a zigzag path to the tree.

4. Gail ate a _____ apple muffin for a snack.

5. One _____ is the same as one cent.

Which word from the word bank did you not use? Write a sentence with the word.

_____

_____

_____

Irregular Words

Name _____

Read and Spell

Read and spell this word to be a better reader.

📖 Read it.	👆 Tap the sounds.
beauty	○○○○○○○

✏️ Color it by sound.

beauty

✏️ Write it.	✏️ Write it again.
_____	_____

📖 Read it.

I love to gaze at the beauty of the sea.

There is so much beauty at the beach.

✏️ Write it in a sentence.

_____

_____

Name

Irregular Words

Read and Spell

Read and spell this word to be a better reader.

📖 Read it.

beautiful

👆 Tap the sounds.

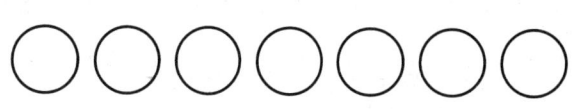

✏️ Color it by sound.

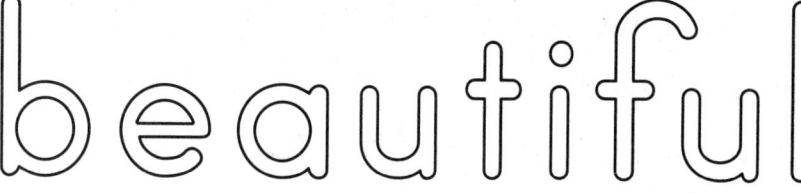

✏️ Write it.

_____

✏️ Write it again.

_____

📖 Read it.

She brushed her teeth and tightened her beautiful raincoat.

✏️ Write it in a sentence.

_____

_____

_____

Decodable Text

Name _____

A Rainy Day

"Please finish your oatmeal," Dad said. "You do not want to miss the bus."

"I'm almost done," Jean told him. "Then I'll brush my teeth and get my backpack. Do you think I need a jacket?"

"It's going to rain," Dad said, "so I think you should wear your raincoat."

A light flashed outside the window, and Jean jumped. "Did you see that?" she asked Dad.

"It must be lightning," Dad said. "And there's the rain! I didn't think it was going to come until lunchtime."

"Well, it didn't wait!" Jean said. "And it's windy as well. Do you see the tree branches blowing?"

"I do," Dad said.

"I'm glad I do not have to walk," Jean added.

"You do have to get to the bus stop," Dad said, "but I can drive you there. If we're quick, you will not get that wet."

"I like that plan," Jean said. She brushed her teeth and tightened her beautiful raincoat. Then she dashed to Dad's van.

▶ Draw a picture that shows what you read in the text.

Name _____

Decodable Text

A Trip to the Sea

Mom and Roan rode on the railway for a day trip to the sea.

"Did you pack minnows for the puffins?" Roan asked.

"I did," Mom said. "I do not know why, but they love them."

"Maybe they are sick of eating squid all the time," Roan said and smiled.

"Could be," Mom chuckled. "I brought lunch for us as well." She held up Roan's rainbow lunch sack and made a picnic.

Mom and Roan each ate a sandwich and a small apple and drank iced tea. Then they walked along the coast to find clamshells and sea glass to take home. They liked to use these beach findings to make crafts to give to people as gifts.

Roan was delighted. "We got fifteen bits of sea glass and eight intact clamshells," he said. "I think I will use most of them to make something beautiful for Gram."

"What a great plan!" Mom said.

▶ Draw a picture that shows what you read in the text.

Name _____

Vocabulary

Power Words: Match

Word Bank

| approached | communicate | deal | figured |
| motioned | potential | selfless | series |

▶ Write the Power Word from *I Am Helen Keller* that best fits each item.

1. When you speak or write a message, you do this. _____

2. Which word means *came close to*? _____

3. Several books that have the same characters are part of this. _____

4. Which word describes how you get along with other people? _____

5. You act like this when you put a friend's needs before your own. _____

6. Which word means *came to understand*? _____

7. You have this because you are working hard toward your future. _____

8. Which word describes how you asked a friend to come closer? _____

Suffixes –ful, –less

A **suffix** is a word part added to the end of a base word. It changes the base word's meaning. The suffix *–ful* means "full of." The suffix *–less* means "without." Use a dictionary to find the meaning of base words that you do not know.

▶ Add the suffix *–ful* or *–less* to the word that is in parentheses ( ) to complete each sentence.

1. I am tired because I had a (sleep) _____ night.

2. A (power) _____ storm kept me awake.

3. My little sister was (fear) _____ of the thunder.

4. I told her that thunder was (harm) _____ .

5. Finally, the storm was over and everything became (peace) _____ .

▶ Add *–ful* or *–less* to each word. Tell what the new word means. If you are unsure about the meaning of the base word, use a dictionary to look up the meaning of the word.

6. end: _____ means _____

7. truth: _____ means _____

Name _____

Comprehension

Text Features

Punctuation marks are **text features** that tell readers when and how long to pause. The dash (—) is a clue to take a short pause. **Ellipses,** or three small dots, mean to pause for a little longer. Words in all capital letters tell you to read that part of the text with more feeling.

▶ Answer the questions about *I Am Helen Keller*.

🔍 **Pages 15 and 18** What does the author want you to do when you get to the dots, or ellipses, on page 15? What does the dash tell you to do? Why do you think the author wants you to pause?

_____

_____

_____

_____

🔍 **Pages 23–24** What do you notice about the words "YOU UNDERSTAND!!" on page 23? How does the author want you to read these words? Why?

_____

_____

_____

_____

_____

Name _____

Vocabulary Strategy

Shades of Meaning

Synonyms are words that mean the same or almost the same thing. **Shades of meaning** are the small differences in meaning between synonyms.

Word Bank

| adore | fantastic | full | good | like | stuffed |

▶ Write the synonyms from the box that best show shades of meaning.

Least	Greater	Greatest
1. _____	packed	_____
2. _____	love	_____
3. _____	great	_____

Word Bank

| hot | boiling | warm |

▶ Choose the best word from the box to complete each sentence.

4. The soup in the pot is _____ on the stove.

5. When the soup is too _____, I wait for it to cool.

6. I like to eat _____ soup on a cold day.

Grade 2 186 Module 7 • Week 1
© Houghton Mifflin Harcourt Publishing Company. All rights reserved.

Name _____

Research Questions

When you **research**, you find out information about a topic. Follow these steps to select questions for a research plan.

1. Write questions about your topic.

2. Remove questions that are off topic.

3. Remove questions that can be answered with *yes* or *no*.

4. Group similar questions together.

Research Prompt: Think of someone from history whose life interests you. What questions do you have about his or her life?

1. Write six questions about your topic. Remember to use your senses to help write your questions.

   My topic: _____

   _____

   _____

Name _____

Research

_____

_____

_____

_____

_____

2. Cross out any questions in your list that are not about your topic.

3. Cross out any questions in your list that can be answered with *yes* or *no*.

4. Group questions about similar things together by writing them in the same box in the chart. Add more boxes if you need them.

My Topic:		
Questions about _____	Questions about _____	Questions about _____

Name _____

r-Controlled Vowel ar

The *r*-controlled vowel *ar* makes the /ar/ sound, as in *farm*.

▶ Write the word that names the picture.

card cart cars	stark start stars

_____	_____
barn bark brain	streak shark shake

_____	_____
cargo carpet carton	grading garden garnish

_____	_____

▶ Write a sentence with one of the words you wrote.

_____

_____

Grade 2   189   Module 7 • Week 2

Name _____

Phonics

r-Controlled Vowel ar

You can spell the /ar/ sound with *ar*, as in *farm*.

▶ Read each clue. Unscramble the word. Write the word from the word bank correctly on the line.

Word Bank

dark   star   yard   party   hard   start   part   spark

1. Not light | k | d | ar | _____

2. Not soft | ar | h | d | _____

3. Land around a home | d | ar | y | _____

4. Light in the night sky | ar | t | s | _____

5. A fun event | y | p | t | ar | _____

6. Starts a flame | ar | k | p | s | _____

7. Same as begin | t | t | s | ar | _____

8. Not a whole | t | ar | p | _____

Grade 2   190   Module 7 • Week 2
© Houghton Mifflin Harcourt Publishing Company. All rights reserved.

Name _____

Irregular Words

Read and Spell

Read and spell this word to be a better reader.

📖 Read it.

heart

👆 Tap the sounds.

○ ○ ○ ○ ○ ○ ○

✏️ Color it by sound.

heart

✏️ Write it.

✏️ Write it again.

📖 Read it.

"I hope you are right," Carmen said as she held her heart.
I can feel my heart beat in my chest.

✏️ Write it in a sentence.

_____

_____

Grade 2

191

Module 7 • Week 2

© Houghton Mifflin Harcourt Publishing Company. All rights reserved.

Name _____

Decodable Text

Carmen's Art

Carmen could sketch and paint anything—people, animals, plants, and landscapes. She sat in the park with art supplies and painted. She used light greens for the grass, dark greens for the trees, and bright red for roses on the bushes. People stopped and watched Carmen as she painted.

"Could you paint us?" someone said.

Carmen gazed up at a man standing with a large, fluffy, white and gray dog.

"I would love to," Carmen replied.

The man and his dog sat still while Carmen painted on a canvas. She flicked an arm this way and that as she made big strokes with the paint. When she was done, she flipped the canvas around, and the man gasped.

"That is spot on!" he said, holding out some bills to pay for the painting. "You are going to be a star one day. I can tell."

"I hope you are right," Carmen said as she held her heart. "I love art so much. And it doesn't feel like a job when you are doing something you love."

▶ Draw a picture that shows what you read in the text.

Name _____

Nan and Pop's Farm

On most weekends, Barb and Karl spend time at Nan and Pop's farm. There are always hard tasks to do, but they have a lot of fun.

Pop posts a chart with all the tasks, and the kids split up the duties.

Barb loads and pulls the hay cart to feed the goats. Karl tidies the barn, cleaning the stalls and brushing the animals there.

Some days, Barb and Karl's cousins come to help. They help to pick the crops and pack them for the farm's shop. And they all help Nan make tarts and jars of jam to sell as well. Barb and Karl like that part the most. Nan's baking is the best, and she always saves tarts for them.

Then, when the work is done and the sky gets dark, they all sit outside and eat the sweet treats as the stars twinkle above them.

Barb and Karl can't think of any other place they'd want to be!

▶ Draw a picture that shows what you read in the text.

Name _____

Power Words: Yes or No?

Word Bank

arrange   current   statements   timeline

▶ Read each sentence. Circle **YES** if the word makes sense or **NO** if it does not. Rewrite the sentence so it makes sense.

1. You should **arrange** flowers on a plate.

    YES   NO

    _____

2. The **current** year begins with the number 2.

    YES   NO

    _____

3. You may answer questions with **statements**.

    YES   NO

    _____

4. A **timeline** shows events in alphabetical order.

    YES   NO

    _____

Name _____

Comprehension

Text Organization

Informational texts have a type of **text organization** that fits the topic and the author's purpose. Authors use **chronological order** when they describe the order of the steps in a process. Clue words like *first*, *then*, *next*, and *finally*—and text features like numbered steps—help readers follow the steps.

▶ Answer the questions about *How to Make a Timeline*.

🔍 Pages 44–45 What do all of the events on Tramayne's timeline have in common? How did Tramayne organize the events on his timeline? What clues help you know?

_____

_____

_____

_____

🔍 Page 46 How are the timeline directions and materials organized? Why did the author organize them like this?

_____

_____

_____

_____

Name _____

Phonics

Phonics Review

The letters *ar* stand for the *r*-controlled vowel sound you hear in the word *farm*.

▶ Choose and write a word in each blank to complete the sentences.

1. Mark wants to grow up to be an _____.

   starch   car   dark   artist

2. He paints with bright yellow and dark _____.

   scarf   scarlet   scalp   scarred

3. Mark says his skill comes _____ from his mom.

   yarn   party   partly   parch

4. She helped Mark _____ his skills.

   sharpen   shark   scar   shadow

5. Mark is painting a red barn with a farm and a beautiful rose _____ .

   marble   part   dark   garden

Generative Vocabulary

Prefix pre-

The **prefix** *pre-* means "before." Use the meaning of the prefix and the **base word** to figure out the meaning of the new word. If you are not sure about the meaning of a base word, you can look the word up in a dictionary.

▶ Use the words in parentheses ( ) to write a word with the prefix *pre-* to complete each sentence.

1. Mom will _____ our clothes before she puts
      (sort before)
   them in the washer.

2. I like to look at the _____ sky.
                           (before dawn)

3. Mr. Muñoz will _____ our plan for the project.
                    (approve before)

4. The sandwiches in the cafeteria were _____ .
                                          (made before)

5. If you _____ the oven, it will be warm
        (heat before)
   when we are ready to cook.

6. Nate _____ for the tickets to the game.
        (paid before)

7. Lila settles into her seat _____ .
                               (before the flight)

Name _____

Vocabulary

Power Words: Draw and Write

Word Bank

ashamed　　　elders　　　overflowing　　　pride

▶ Draw a picture or write words that will help you remember each Power Word from *The Stories He Tells: The Story of Joseph Bruchac.* Try to write more than you draw.

1. ashamed

2. elders

3. overflowing

4. pride

Name _____

Comprehension

Author's Purpose

Authors write to **persuade**, **inform**, or **entertain**. How can you find the author's purpose? First, look for clues about the genre. Then, ask questions about what you read and find answers.

▶ Answer the questions about *The Stories He Tells: The Story of Joseph Bruchac*.

🔍 Pages 52–54 What clues about the genre of this text help you know what type of text you are reading?

_____
_____
_____
_____

🔍 Pages 58–60 What do you think is the author's purpose for writing this text? What makes this author's perspective about Joseph Bruchac special?

_____
_____
_____
_____

Name _____

Phonics

r-Controlled Vowels are, air, ear

The r-controlled vowel *are* stands for the /air/ sound, as in *share*.
The r-controlled vowel *air* stands for the /air/ sound, as in *hair*.
The r-controlled vowel *ear* can stand for the /air/ sound, as in *bear*.

▶ Write the word that names the picture.

bar bear bare	square stare star
care car chair	pear pair park
hardware dairy airplane	hare hair harp

Name _____

Phonics

Homophones

Homophones are words that sound the same but have different spellings and meanings. *Hair* and *hare* are homophones.

▶ Read each word. Use the word bank to find a homophone for each word. Write the homophone on the line.

Word Bank

pear
meat
weigh
mane
tail
bare
too

Homophone Pairs

two _____

main _____

bear _____

way _____

meet _____

tale _____

pair _____

▶ Choose one pair of homophones. Write a sentence with each word in the pair.

_____

_____

Grade 2

Module 7 • Week 3

© Houghton Mifflin Harcourt Publishing Company. All rights reserved.

Irregular Words

Name _____

Read and Spell

Read and spell this word to be a better reader.

📖 Read it.	👆 Tap the sounds.
toward	○○○○○○○

✏️ Color it by sound.

toward

✏️ Write it.	✏️ Write it again.
_____	_____

📖 Read it.

Do not move quickly toward them.

The bear went toward the cave.

✏️ Write it in a sentence.

_____

_____

Grade 2   201   Module 7 • Week 3

Irregular Words

Name _____

Read and Spell

Read and spell this word to be a better reader.

📖 Read it.

together

👆 Tap the sounds.

○ ○ ○ ○ ○ ○ ○

✏️ Color it by sound.

together

✏️ Write it.

_____

✏️ Write it again.

_____

📖 Read it.

"You could pile your hair together into a bun,"
Dad said.
We can sit together on the airplane.

✏️ Write it in a sentence.

_____

_____

Decodable Text

The Lost Brush

Robin's hair was full of tangles, and she couldn't find the brush.

"Did you check upstairs?" Robin's dad asked. "It must be up there."

Robin checked in the bins and by the bed. She checked in the bag of bath supplies and by the sink.

"I didn't see it anywhere, Dad. Plus, I'm in a rush. I do not want to be late for art class. By the way, Clare is coming home with me when class is done for the day."

"OK, let's take care of your hair," Dad said. "Do you want to put it in a ponytail?"

"I would like to wear a ponytail, but I still need the brush to do one."

"You could pile your hair together into a bun," Dad said.

"I'll try the bun. Thanks, Dad," Robin said. "But it would be easier if I had the brush."

"Check it out, Robin!" Dad said. "By the chair! It's the brush!"

▶ Draw a picture that shows what you read in the text.

Name _____

Taking a Hike

You can do a lot to plan for a hike!

You can read about the trails you will go on. You can decide what to wear based on when and where you will go.

You do not need to dress with flair on a hike. And you should NOT plan to hike in bare feet, not even on a dare.

You should pack things you will need for cold or hot times. You should pack extra pairs of socks in case your feet get wet and a raincoat in case it rains.

You should bring some snacks that are light and easy to pack, such as pears and trail mix.

If you are going to a place that's very wild, you might bring flares in case you get lost. And you should know what to do in case you see a wild animal, such as a snake or a bear. Do not move quickly toward them.

Planning is the key to a safe and fun hike!

▶ Draw a picture that shows what you read in the text.

Name _____

Power Words: Match

Word Bank

| allowed | alone | dared | deserved |
| reminding | secret | starlit | whir |

▶ Write the Power Word from *Drum Dream Girl* that best fits each item.

1. Which word describes a nighttime sky? _____

2. This describes you when you are all by yourself. _____

3. You may whisper this into your friend's ear. _____

4. When someone tells you again, they are doing this. _____

5. Which word means *was brave enough to do something*? _____

6. A fan and a car's engine may both make this noise. _____

7. Which word means the opposite of *had not earned*? _____

8. If someone says something is okay to do, it is this. _____

Name _____

Comprehension

Setting

The **setting** of a story is where and when a story or poem takes place. Authors give **details**, or small bits of information, to **describe** the setting. Readers can ask, "Why is the setting important to the story?" to understand what is happening in the story and why.

▶ Answer the questions about *Drum Dream Girl*.

🔍 Pages 66–71 Where does the drum dream girl live? What clues in the illustrations tell you more about her home?

_____
_____
_____
_____
_____

🔍 Pages 72–78 Where does the girl go? Why are these different places important to the poem?

_____
_____
_____
_____
_____

Name _____

Phonics Review

The *r*-controlled vowels *are, air,* and *ear* can stand for the /air/ sound, as in the words *share, hair,* and *bear.*

Homophones are words that sound the same, but are spelled differently and have different meanings, like the words *hare* and *hair.*

▶ Choose and write a word in each blank to complete the sentences.

1. I watched the _____ eat the ripe _____.

       bare   pear   bear   pair

2. We went the long _____ so that we could drive by the _____.

       weigh   sea   see   way

3. We got the tickets to the _____ in the _____ today.

       male   mail   fair   fare

4. I stepped on the _____ pin with my _____.

       tow   hare   hair   toe

5. We take the _____ to get on to the _____.

       plain   stairs   stares   plane

Name _____

Generative Vocabulary

Compound Words

Compound words are made up of two smaller words. Knowing the smaller words can help you read, spell, and know the meaning of the compound word. Use a dictionary to check if your meaning is correct.

▶ Draw a line to divide each compound word into two smaller words. Then write the meaning of the compound word. Use a dictionary to check if your meaning is correct.

1. sunrise _____

2. backpack _____

3. raincoat _____

4. lunchroom _____

5. mailbox _____

▶ Read the word pairs and write the compound word on the line.

6. base, ball _____

7. hall, way _____

8. sea, horse _____

Grade 2 206 Module 7 • Week 3
© Houghton Mifflin Harcourt Publishing Company. All rights reserved.

r-Controlled Vowel or

An *r*-controlled vowel sound is not short or long. The *r* changes the way a vowel sounds. The grapheme *or* can stand for the *r*-controlled vowel sound you hear in the word *fork*.

▶ Write the word that names the picture. Circle the letters that stand for the *r*-controlled vowel sound you hear in *corn*.

cord corn cork	fork fort farm
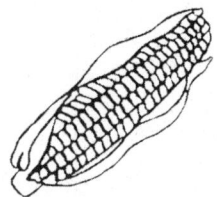	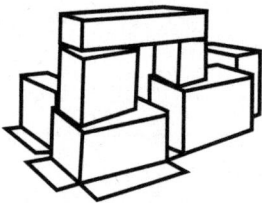
shorts scorn scorch	seashore seahorse seaport

form force fork	torch thorn torn

Name _____

r-Controlled Vowels ore, our

The graphemes *ore* and *our* can stand for the /or/ sound, as in the words *tore* and *four*. When we hear /or/ at the end of a word, it is usually spelled with *ore*.

▶ Read each sentence. Write the word from the word bank that best completes each sentence.

Word Bank

chore
tore
your
court
store
wore
shore
snore
course
four

1. We like to jog along the _____ when we go to the beach.

2. Do I _____ when I sleep?

3. I had a party with _____ of my best pals.

4. I got a snack when we went to the _____.

5. It is kind to be nice to _____ siblings.

6. I _____ the cloth into two parts.

7. I like to run on the basketball _____.

8. My mom teaches a _____, or class, on art.

▶ Write a sentence with a word from the word bank you did not use.

_____

_____

Grade 2
Module 8 • Week 1

Name _____

Phonics

Phonics Review

The *r*-controlled vowel *or* can stand for the /or/ sound, as in *fork*.
The *r*-controlled vowel *ore* stands for the /or/ sound, as in *tore*.
The *r*-controlled vowel *our* can stand for the /or/ sound, as in *four*.

▶ Choose and write a word to complete each sentence.

1. The Morris family went to the _____ one morning.

   season   seashore   seahorse

2. "Do not _____ sunscreen!" Mom said.

   forget   four   forgive

3. Morgan _____ a cap to block the sun.

   wore   war   won

4. He makes a sand _____ with a flag on top.

   fort   fork   ford

5. Cora plans to _____ the beach and pick up shells.

   express   export   explore

6. The family plays a game on the sand volleyball _____ .

   court   source   your

Grade 2   209   Module 8 • Week 1
© Houghton Mifflin Harcourt Publishing Company. All rights reserved.

Name _____

Irregular Words

Read and Spell

Read and spell this word to be a better reader.

📖 Read it.

someone

👆 Tap the sounds.
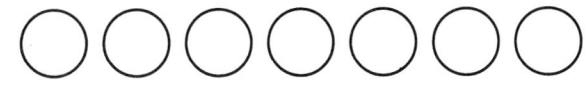

✏️ Color it by sound.

✏️ Write it.

_____

✏️ Write it again.

_____

📖 Read it.

If it is hard, you can ask someone for more resources to get the task done!
Can someone help me find the cord for my laptop?

✏️ Write it in a sentence.

_____

_____

Grade 2 210 Module 8 • Week 1
© Houghton Mifflin Harcourt Publishing Company. All rights reserved.

Name _____

Irregular Words

Read and Spell

Read and spell this word to be a better reader.

📖 Read it.　　　　　　　　　👆 Tap the sounds.

everyone　　○○○○○○○

✏️ Color it by sound.

everyone

✏️ Write it.　　　　　　　　　✏️ Write it again.

_____　　　　　　　_____

📖 Read it.

"We are still sailing north!" I yelled to everyone.

Everyone in my family helps with the chores.

✏️ Write it in a sentence.

_____

_____

Grade 2　　　　　210a　　　　　Module 8 • Week 1

Name _____

Decodable Text

Sailing for Home

I was born to sail the open sea. There is nothing like taking in the wide skies and fresh breezes out on the sea.

But my mates and I have sailed for weeks without landing. We are getting sort of sick of it.

I watched Thor eat a stale cake made of corn. Corn cakes are all we have left to eat.

"It's so hard," he sighed. "It broke my fork."

"I miss grass," added Orla. "And my horse."

That night, we hit a big storm. Wind rocked the ship back and forth. It put out my torch. I could not see. I could just make out the ship's horn.

But when the sun rose, all was bright again. Thor fixed a torn sail as I checked my compass.

"We are still sailing north!" I yelled to everyone.

Thor swung from cord to cord up high in the ship's masts. "I see the port," he cried.

Orla screeched like a gull. "Yay for land!"

▶ Draw a picture that shows what you read in the text.

Name _____

Hack Your Chores

Do your chores feel like a bore? Do they make you snore? These four tips can help!

1. Go to a store. Pick out some fun decor that matches your space. It can make doing chores more fun!
2. Clean up your space! Put away things that may distract you.
3. Plan short breaks from your chores. You can tell yourself, "When I finish this task, I will pour myself something to drink." Or you might say, "While I clean for fourteen minutes, I will play some music."
4. Ask yourself why you feel bored. Does the chore feel easy or hard? If it is hard, you can ask someone for more resources to get the task done!

You may have to try lots of things before you adore your chores. But keep going. You can do it!

▶ Draw a picture that shows what you read in the text.

Name _____

Vocabulary

Power Words: Match

Word Bank

| fuels | minerals | moisten | process |
| provides | seedlings | spiky | sprout |

▶ Write the Power Word from *Experiment with What a Plant Needs to Grow* that best fits each item.

1. To do this to a sponge, I would dip it into a pail of water. _____

2. Which word describes something that is sharp and pointy? _____

3. What do all plants and animals need to grow? _____

4. These are young plants. _____

5. Which word describes the action of giving a thing power? _____

6. You follow steps in order to complete this. _____

7. This is the action of a new plant breaking through the soil. _____

8. Which word means the opposite of *takes away*? _____

Name _____

Generative Vocabulary

Inflections –s, –es

The endings –s and –es added to the end of a **singular noun** makes it **plural**, or changes the number of something. The ending –s or –es added to the end of a **verb** shows that an action is happening now, or in the present.

▶ Add –s or –es to the word in bold. If the word you changed is a noun, circle *Noun*. If the word you changed is a verb, circle *Verb*.

1. The hungry bird **search** _____ for a worm to eat. Noun   Verb

2. Do you know why some **animal** _____ sleep so much? Noun   Verb

3. The cook **mix** _____ together eggs, flour, and milk. Noun   Verb

4. He turned on all the light **switch** _____ in the house. Noun   Verb

5. Martin washed two **cup** _____ in the sink. Noun   Verb

6. The dentist gave us new **toothbrush** _____ . Noun   Verb

7. Didi **play** _____ with her friends every Saturday. Noun   Verb

8. Nana **get** _____ her mail at the same time every day. Noun   Verb

Name _____

Comprehension

Text Organization

Text organization is the way an author shares information so readers will understand it. Authors organize texts to fit the topic and their purpose for writing. One way to organize text is by **cause** and **effect**. A cause is why something happens, and an effect is what happens as a result of a cause.

▶ Answer the questions about *Experiment with What a Plant Needs to Grow*.

🔍 Pages 105–108 What caused the seeds in the cotton balls to not grow well? What was the effect of giving the seeds no water? What do you notice about how the text is organized?

_____

_____

_____

_____

🔍 Page 111 What is the cause of the leaves starting to wilt? What is the effect of putting petroleum jelly on the bottom of the leaves? Why do you think the author organizes the text around causes and effects?

_____

_____

_____

_____

Name _____

Vocabulary Strategy

Reference Sources

When you are reading, you may see a word you do not know. Use a **dictionary** or a **glossary** to find out the word's meaning, how to say it, and how to spell it. Words in a dictionary or a glossary are listed in **alphabetical order**.

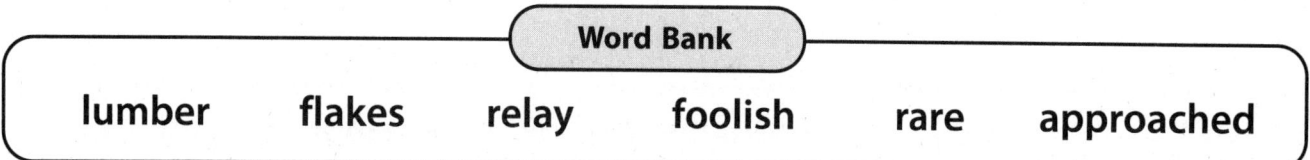

▶ Write the words from the box in alphabetical order.

1. _____   4. _____

2. _____   5. _____

3. _____   6. _____

▶ Look up these words in a glossary or dictionary: *frigid, beamed*. Write the words next to the picture that shows the word's meaning. Check that you spelled each word correctly.

7.    _____

8.    _____

Name _____

Choose and Use Sources

Before writing a book, authors have to research information about their topic. Research sources include **experts**, **primary sources**, and **secondary sources**. Sources can also be print or digital. Print sources include books, pictures, and magazines. Websites and videos are digital sources.

Types of Sources	
Experts	People who know information about a topic because of their job or education
Primary Sources	Original documents, such as diaries, interviews, or research results
Secondary Sources	Books, reports, or articles that someone wrote using primary sources

1. Would a letter written by Abraham Lincoln be a primary or secondary source? _____

2. A person writes a new book about pine trees using the research results someone else wrote. Is the new book a primary or secondary source? _____

Name _____

Research

Put a checkmark next to sources you would use to answer the research question below. If it's a source you would use, write if it is an expert, primary, or secondary source.

Research question: How do plants use sunlight to make food?

1. Research by a scientist who studies plants

   ☐ Type of source: _____

2. A book about how to stay safe in the sun

   ☐ Type of source: _____

3. A person who teaches others about plants

   ☐ Type of source: _____

4. A website about plants that someone made using primary sources

   ☐ Type of source: _____

Authors list the sources they use when researching a topic. Find two sources with information about plants. Then write your sources on the lines below.

1. Name of author _____

   Title of source _____

2. Name of author _____

   Title of source _____

r-Controlled Vowels er, ir, ur

An *r*-controlled vowel sound is not short or long. The *r* changes the way a vowel sounds. The graphemes *er*, *ir*, and *ur* can stand for the /er/ sound, as in the words *ladder*, *bird*, and *fur*.

▶ Write the word that names the picture. Then circle the grapheme that stands for the *r*-controlled vowel sound /er/ in each word.

turnip   twirling   tiger

_____

third   turtle   term

_____

perch   parts   purse

_____

iceberg   sunburn   birthday

_____

girls   gerbils   germs

_____

birdcage   blackbird   surprise

_____

Name _____

Phonics

r-Controlled Vowels eer, ear

You can spell the /ēr/ sound with the graphemes *eer*, as in *deer*, and *ear*, as in *ear*.

▶ Write the word from the word bank that best completes each sentence.

Word Bank

deer
clear
tear
hear
peer
cheer
smear
steer
volunteer

1. My family comes to _____ for me at my swim meets.

2. The lake is so _____ you can see to the bottom!

3. I like to _____ to help clean the park on the weekends.

4. I watched the _____ take a drink from the river.

5. The paint will _____ if you touch it before it dries.

6. Did you _____ the thunder?

7. I am going to learn how to _____ the car one day.

▶ Write a sentence with a word from the word bank that you did not use.

_____

_____

Name _____

Irregular Words

Read and Spell

Read and spell this word to be a better reader.

| 📖 Read it.

learn | 👆 Tap the sounds.

◯ ◯ ◯ ◯ ◯ ◯ ◯ |

✏️ Color it by sound.

learn

| ✏️ Write it.

_____ | ✏️ Write it again.

_____ |

📖 Read it.

Put on an old shirt, because it's time to learn to plant some seeds in the earth.
I love to learn new things in class every day!

✏️ Write it in a sentence.

_____

_____

Grade 2 220 Module 8 • Week 2
© Houghton Mifflin Harcourt Publishing Company. All rights reserved.

Irregular Words

Name _____

Read and Spell

Read and spell this word to be a better reader.

📖 Read it.

👆 Tap the sounds.

✏️ Color it by sound.

✏️ Write it.

_____

✏️ Write it again.

_____

📖 Read it.

Earth is the third planet from the sun.

What things can we do to help protect the earth?

✏️ Write it in a sentence.

_____

_____

Irregular Words

Name _____

Read and Spell

Read and spell this word to be a better reader.

📖 Read it.   👆 Tap the sounds.

early   ○ ○ ○ ○ ○ ○ ○

✏️ Color it by sound.

early

✏️ Write it.   ✏️ Write it again.

_____   _____

📖 Read it.

It must be early spring!

It is best to come early and not be late!

✏️ Write it in a sentence.

_____

_____

Name _____

Decodable Text

Seeds in the Dirt

Are there buds on that tree? Did a baby bird just chirp? It must be early spring! Put on an old shirt, because it's time to learn to plant some seeds in the earth.

First, make a line of seeds. Then, turn the dirt. You will not see much at first. But in time, little curls of green will burst up.

Do not let your seedlings die of thirst! Give them lots to drink. If it does not rain for days, squirt them with a hose. Do not let them burn in the sun.

Do you want plants to serve for lunch? Plant some bean or pea seeds.

Do you have a spot with lots of sun? Plant turnips. Turnips like sun.

Do you need more shade? Big plants like fir trees are hard to start from seeds. But you can plant a sapling, or little tree. Birds will love to perch on it!

▶ Draw a picture that shows what you read in the text.

Name _____

Decodable Text

Greer's Big Race

Greer peers at the clock. It is time to wake up! The big sled race is today. She has been training for weeks.

Greer puts on her snow pants and coat. She gets her sled. She takes her place at the top of the hill next to Greg.

"No one sleds as fast as me," Greg sneers.

Greer peers into the trees. She watches a deer stop in the snow. She will not let Greg scare her.

One, two, three, go! Greg and Greer steer the sleds. Greg is right next to Greer, but Greer does not see him. She does not see the trees. She does not see the deer. It all turns to a blur as she picks up speed.

When Greer comes to a stop, a huge cheer fills the air. People are yelling her name. "Yay, Greer! Greer wins! Three cheers for Greer!"

▶ Draw a picture that shows what you read in the text.

Name _____

Vocabulary

Power Words: Draw and Write

Word Bank

| plenty | swipe | whacked | whimpered |

▶ Draw a picture or write words that will help you remember each Power Word from *Jack and the Beanstalk*. Try to write more than you draw.

1. plenty

2. swipe

3. whacked

4. whimpered

Grade 2
© Houghton Mifflin Harcourt Publishing Company. All rights reserved.

Module 8 • Week 2

Name _____

Comprehension

Figurative Language

Literal language uses words that mean exactly what they say. **Figurative language** uses words that mean something different from what they say. Three types of figurative language are:

- **simile:** compares two different things using the word *like* or *as*
- **idiom:** words that mean something different from their everyday meaning
- **alliteration:** a pattern of words with the same first sounds

▶ Answer the questions about *Jack and the Beanstalk*.

🔍 Pages 118–119 How does the simile "held like a treasure" help you understand how Jack feels about the beans? What does Jack's mother mean when she says the beans "won't put food on the table?"

_____

_____

_____

🔍 Pages 124 What does the author mean when she says Jack "leapt up the beanstalk like a mountain goat"?

_____

_____

_____

Name _____

Phonics Review

The graphemes *er, ir,* and *ur* can stand for the /er/ sound.
The graphemes *eer* and *ear* can stand for the /ēr/ sound.

▶ Choose and write two words to complete each sentence.

1. Ginger is going on her _____ big trip to the sea to learn to _____ .

   deer   first   fear   surf

2. As she gets closer to the beach, she can _____ the seagulls and see the _____, beautiful waves.

   hear   bird   clear   fern

3. She puts on her swim _____ and sunscreen, then meets the _____ that will help her learn to surf.

   smear   volunteer   blur   shirt

4. Ginger puts on more _____, and then jumps into the sea with a big _____.

   term   gear   cheer   nurse

5. Her lesson was a _____, but by the end Ginger can float and steer on the waves with no _____!

   blur   chirp   clerk   fear

Name _____

Generative Vocabulary

Prefix mis-

The **prefix** *mis-* means "wrong." Use the meaning of the prefix and the **base word** to figure out the meaning of the new word. If you are not sure about the meaning of a base word, look it up in a dictionary.

▶ Add the prefix *mis-* to each word. Write the new word on the line. Then write what the word means.

1. mis- + judge = _____ means _____

2. mis- + take = _____ means _____
   _____

3. mis- + match = _____ means _____
   _____

Word Bank

misled   mispronounce   misprint

▶ Complete each sentence with a word from the box.

4. Did I _____ your name?

5. The directions _____ Juan to believe he put the toy together correctly.

6. Because of a _____ on the map, we did not go the right way.

Grade 2
© Houghton Mifflin Harcourt Publishing Company. All rights reserved.

Module 8 • Week 2

Name _____

Vocabulary

Power Words: Yes or No?

Word Bank

adorable   glanced   hauling   oversized

▶ Read each sentence. Circle **YES** if the word makes sense or **NO** if it does not. Rewrite the sentence so it makes sense.

1. A wagon is good for **hauling** heavy things.

    YES   NO

    _____

2. We **glanced** at the picture for a long time.

    YES   NO

    _____

3. An **oversized** shirt feels very loose when you put it on.

    YES   NO

    _____

4. It is hard to like an **adorable** puppy.

    YES   NO

    _____

Name _____

Comprehension

Characters

The **characters** are the people or animals in a story. **External traits** are what a character looks like on the outside. **Internal traits** describe a character's personality, or what he or she thinks and feels.

▶ Answer the questions about *Jackie and the Beanstalk.*

🔍 Pages 134–136 How does Jackie respond when the woman describes the special beans? What does that tell you about Jackie?

_____

_____

_____

_____

🔍 Pages 138–139 How does Jackie feel when she realizes Mr. Fefifofum thinks she stole the harp? Tell how you know. What does she do to feel better? What do these actions tell you about Jackie?

_____

_____

_____

_____

Name _____

Phonics

r-Controlled Vowels or, ar

We know that the *r*-controlled vowel *or* can stand for the /or/ sound. We also know that the *r*-controlled vowel *ar* can stand for the /ar/ sound. Both of these graphemes can also stand for the /er/ sound, as in *worm* and *dollar*.

▶ Write the word that names the picture. Then circle the grapheme that stands for the *r*-controlled vowel sound /er/ sound in each word.

world work worth	doctor dollar collar
 _____	 _____
worst worm work	solar dollar doctor
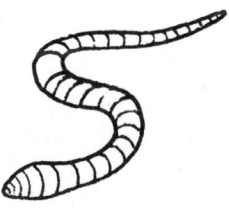 _____	 _____
collar lunar polar	tractor actor pillar
 _____	 _____

Grade 2 · 228 · Module 8 • Week 3

Phonics

Name _____

r-Controlled Vowels *or, ar*

The *r*-controlled vowels *or* and *ar* can both stand for the /er/ sound, as in *worm* and *dollar*.

▶ Write the word from the word bank that best completes each sentence.

Word Bank

nectar
worth
grammar
pillar
word
world
solar
worst
actors

1. I had the _____ cold I had ever had!

2. Bees drink the _____ from the plants.

3. The _____ perform their best on stage.

4. _____ is the study of how words work.

5. The vendor can tell me what this is _____ .

6. My mom flies airplanes all over the _____ !

7. I taped the note to the _____ so people can see it.

8. _____ energy comes from the sun.

▶ Write a sentence for the word in the word bank you did not use.

_____

_____

Irregular Words

Name _____

Read and Spell

Read and spell this word to be a better reader.

| 📖 Read it. **their** | 👆 Tap the sounds. ○ ○ ○ ○ ○ ○ ○ |

✏️ Color it by sound.

their

| ✏️ Write it. _____ | ✏️ Write it again. _____ |

📖 Read it.

Around the world, people use their money to the things they want and need.
We went to their new house for the party.

✏️ Write it in a sentence.

_____

_____

Name _____

Dollar Bills

If you work, you might have some dollars in your pocket or piggy bank.

Around the world, people use their money to buy the things they want and need. Words for money differ from place to place. In the United States, people can use dollars and cents.

One dollar bill is worth the same as one hundred cents. That means one dollar is worth the same as one hundred pennies, twenty nickels, or ten dimes.

There are also bills that are worth two, five, ten, twenty, fifty, and one hundred dollars. When people spend dollars, the bills travel from place to place. Someone may give bills to a store to buy something. Then the store may put the bills in a bank. And someone may get those bills from the bank.

In time, dollar bills can get worn out. But more bills are printed each day to take their place.

▶ Draw a picture that shows what you read in the text.

Name _____

Decodable Text

The Worst Morning

"Kelly, are you set?" Mom called. "You do not want to be late for your first day of work."

"I am getting dressed, Mom. Can you cut this tag off my shirt?" Kelly asked.

As Mom cut the tag off, she spotted a stain on the collar. "There is a big spot on the collar."

"What?" Kelly said. "I just bought this shirt! It was on sale for ten dollars, but why is it stained?"

Just then, Buddy barked from outside.

"Great," Kelly groaned. "It's pouring buckets."

Mom got Kelly a clean shirt from the cellar. "I hope this fits," she said.

As Kelly slipped the shirt on, Mom let Buddy in.

Buddy was quick! He slipped right out of his collar and jumped up at Kelly with four muddy feet.

"This is the worst morning," Kelly cried. "I hope my first day of work is better than this!"

▶ Draw a picture that shows what you read in the text.

Name _____

Vocabulary

Power Words: Match

Word Bank

| attack | extra | nasty | poke |
| prickles | sensitive | sharp | thorns |

▶ Write the Power Word from *Don't Touch Me!* that best fits each item.

1. This word means the opposite of *pleasant*. _____

2. Which word means that you give a quick response? _____

3. A wolf will do this to another animal. _____

4. Which word means to *jab into suddenly*? _____

5. When you have more than the usual amount, you have this. _____

6. An animal will feel pain if it has these stuck in its paw. _____

7. You should wear gloves when you touch a rose that has these. _____

8. This word can be used to describe a sewing needle. _____

Grade 2

Module 8 • Week 3

Name _____

Comprehension

Text Organization

Text organization is the way an author organizes a text to help readers understand the information. Texts organized by **cause** and **effect** describe how one event leads to another event. A cause is something that happens. An effect is what happens as a result of the cause.

▶ Answer the questions about *Don't Touch Me!*

🔍 Page 147 How does the text help you understand the connection between these plants? What clue does the author give to help you understand the effect of touching these plants?

_____

_____

_____

_____

_____

🔍 Pages 148–149 What causes and effects do you see on these pages? Why did the author organize the selection this way?

_____

_____

_____

_____

_____

Grade 2

Phonics Review

The *r*-controlled vowel *or* can stand for the /er/ sound.
The *r*-controlled vowel *ar* can also stand for the /er/ sound.

▶ Choose and write one word to complete each sentence.

1. Last weekend, my mom was a _____ at a farmer's market.

    collar   cedar   pillar   vendor

2. She _____ hard all week to get things all set for the event.

    worth   worked   worst   word

3. First, she decided she would sell her homemade peach and mango _____ .

    grammar   worm   nectar   dollar

4. Then, she had to decide what her items are _____, so she could give them a price.

    worth   world   doctor   actor

5. My mom was one of the most _____ vendors at the market!

    cellar   popular   lunar   polar

Name _____

Generative Vocabulary

Prefix dis-

The **prefix** *dis–* means "not" or "the opposite of." Use the meaning of the prefix and the **base word** to figure out the meaning of the new word. Look up base words you do not know in a dictionary.

▶ Write a word with the prefix *dis–* for each definition.

1. to not approve of: _____

2. to not trust: _____

3. not continued: _____

Word Bank

disbelief   disorder   displeased

▶ Write a word from the box to complete each sentence.

4. The riders were _____ because the bus was late.

5. Too many cooks led to _____ in the kitchen.

6. They gasped with _____ as they watched the magic show.

Grade 2
235
Module 8 • Week 3

Name _____

Phonics

V/CV Syllable Division Pattern

When a word has one consonant between two vowels, the Tiger Rule tells us to divide after the first vowel (*ti-ger*).

▶ Draw a line (/) to divide each word into syllables.

locate	lazy	students
frozen	silent	broken

▶ Use the words above to complete the sentences.

1. Ice can be made from anything that can be

   _____ .

2. I have never _____ a bone, but my older sister did while playing hockey one time.

3. Both my dog and my cat like to be _____ and lay on the sofa all day.

4. I must be as _____ as I can be when we play hide and seek!

5. Can she _____ the place we need to go on the map?

6. I try to be one of the best _____ in class each day.

Name _____

VC/V Syllable Division Pattern

Phonics

When a word has one consonant between two vowels and the Tiger Rule does not work, the Camel Rule tells us to divide after the consonant (*cam-el*).

▶ Draw a line (/) to divide each word in the word bank into syllables. Then look at each picture. Write the word from the word bank that best fits each picture.

Word Bank

cabin   wagon   camel   lemon   salad   planet

1. _____

2. _____

3. _____

4. _____

5. _____

6. _____

Grade 2   237   Module 9 • Week 1
© Houghton Mifflin Harcourt Publishing Company. All rights reserved.

Phonics

Name _____

Phonics Review

When a word has one consonant between two vowels, the Tiger Rule tells us to divide after the first vowel (*ti-ger*).

When a word has one consonant between two vowels and the Tiger Rule does not work, the Camel Rule tells us to divide after the consonant (*cam-el*).

▶ Read each word, then draw a line (/) to divide each word into syllables. Then write the word that best completes each sentence on the line.

1. **music   dragon**

   I love to dance to all kinds of _____ .

2. **planet   robot**

   I wish I had a _____ to help with my chores!

3. **frozen   wagon**

   The lake must be _____ in order to go ice fishing.

4. **finish   protect**

   We can help to _____ the earth by recycling.

5. **pupils   petals**

   The tulip had beautiful pink _____ .

6. **comet   bacon**

   We watched the _____ fly across the sky!

Name _____

Decodable Text

The Bridge

"I love camp," Lorin said.

"I like our mentor, Mabel," Zoe said.

The kids wore navy blue shirts and visors to shade the sun.

Mabel showed them the way to do things at the camp. They dashed in and out of the trees like jungle tigers. They scaled the rock wall like spiders. But they saved crossing the hanging bridge till later in the summer. They didn't think they could face the bridge just yet.

Then, on the very last day of camp, Zoe and Lorin agreed to cross the bridge. Mabel helped them. They inched over it, and something splashed below.

"It is a gator!" Lorin cried.

"You are silly," Zoe said.

When they reached the cedar trees on the other side, they both let out a huge sigh. They had never felt so brave.

"Super job!" Mabel said with a huge grin.

"Thanks, Mabel," Lorin said. "That wasn't so bad after all. I can't wait to do it again."

▶ Draw a picture that shows what you read in the text.

Name _____

Mars Rovers

Mars is a cold and rocky planet in our solar system. It is called the Red Planet. Red dirt covers the planet. It has ditches that may have been made by rivers a long time ago.

Over time, the United States has sent five rovers to Mars.

A rover is a robot with six wheels, but it does not have a driver inside it. It has cameras and computers to record data. Someone on Earth programs the rover to know what to do and where to go.

Rovers drive around Mars, explore the surface, and study the rocks. The rovers check for clues about liquid or life that existed there.

The rovers have not returned to Earth, but they have sent data back. They have sent data about liquid under ice caps and in the air as vapor.

Some people hope that one day they will be able to visit Mars. Time will tell if that is possible!

▶ Draw a picture that shows what you read in the text.

Name _____

Vocabulary

Power Words: Match

Word Bank

| coast | crouches | flock | mingles |
| prances | route | trills | wobbly |

▶ Write the Power Word from *The Long, Long Journey* that best fits each item.

1. Which word means *moves with high steps*? _____

2. This is another word for *mixes together*. _____

3. It is the path you travel from your house to your school. _____

4. This is another word for how a bird sings. _____

5. Which word means the opposite of *steady*? _____

6. If your friend bends his knees to get low, he does this. _____

7. This is a word that names a large group of birds. _____

8. It is where the ocean meets the land. _____

Name _____

Generative Vocabulary

Words That Name Places

A **noun** is a word that names a person, place, or thing. Nouns that name places tell where something is happening. Use a dictionary to find the meaning of nouns you do not know.

▶ Circle the noun that names a place in each word group.

1. sheep   corn   field
2. truck   house   hay
3. farmer   hen   kitchen
4. town   mailbox   deer
5. visitor   airport   child
6. hillside   teacher   peanut

▶ Complete each sentence with a noun that names a place.

7. Many people live in a _____ .

8. We went to the _____ to read books.

9. When I arrive at _____ , I say hello to my friends.

10. I enjoy spending a day at the _____ .

Grade 2
242
Module 9 • Week 1
© Houghton Mifflin Harcourt Publishing Company. All rights reserved.

Name _____

Comprehension

Text Organization

Authors use **text organization** to help readers find information easily. A text organized by **chronological order** tells about events in order. This helps readers understand what happened first, next, and last. It also helps them understand how one event connects to the next.

▶ Answer the questions about *The Long, Long Journey*.

🔍 Pages 170–174 What does the little female learn to do on pages 170–174? In what order does the author describe these events? Why do you think she did this?

_____
_____
_____
_____

🔍 Pages 176–179 In your own words, tell what happens during the godwits' long journey. How does the way the text is organized support the author's purpose for writing?

_____
_____
_____
_____

Name _____

Vocabulary Strategy

Context Clues

When you come to a word you do not know, use **context clues** to figure out its meaning. Look around the word you do not know for clues about what it means.

▶ Read each sentence. Circle the clues that help you know the meaning of the underlined word. Then write the meaning on the line.

1. Helen wants to work as a park ranger. She thinks that it will be an exciting career.

   _____

2. She uses an axe to hack branches and brush.

   _____

3. The towering mountains seem to touch the sky.

   _____

4. The paths are hard to see at night. So the workers hold lanterns when they walk on the trails.

   _____

Name _____

Digital Reference Sources

Media Literacy

You can look up unfamiliar words in a dictionary or glossary. These resources list words in **alphabetical order**. Glossaries or dictionaries may also be **digital resources**, or online tools.

▶ Read the passage. Then answer the questions.

American Bird Migration

Some birds stay close to home. Others travel long distances. Birds that travel are said to *migrate*.

A <u>permanent</u> <u>resident</u> does not migrate at all. You may see those birds all year long.

Birds that migrate a short distance do not go far. They might move up and down a mountain.

Some birds migrate a medium distance. They may <u>span</u> several states as they fly.

Birds that migrate a long distance go far. Some birds may take a long <u>route</u> from the United States to South America.

Media Literacy

Name _____

1. Write the underlined words in alphabetical order.

   _____

2. Look up *permanent* in a digital dictionary. Write the first meaning you find.

   _____

   _____

3. Look up *resident* in a digital dictionary. Write the first meaning you find.

   _____

   _____

4. Which of the underlined words has two possible pronunciations?

   _____

5. Look up the word *span* in both a digital and a print dictionary. Compare what you found.

   _____

   _____

   _____

   _____

   _____

Name _____

Phonics

Vowel Team oo and vowel u /o͝o/

You can spell the /o͝o/ sound with the grapheme *oo*, as in *book*, and with *u*, as in *push*.

▶ Read each clue. Unscramble the tiles. Write the word from the word bank correctly on the line.

Word Bank

push   books   foot   hoof   cook   nook   hood   wood   pull   shook

1. We can read them.   k s oo b   _____

2. Do this on a stove.   oo k c   _____

3. A horse's foot   f oo h   _____

4. A small corner   oo k n   _____

5. Part of a jacket.   oo h d   _____

6. Do this to a button.   u sh p   _____

7. It comes from trees.   d w oo   _____

8. Do this to a rope   ll p u   _____

9. Part of your body   oo t f   _____

Grade 2   247   Module 9 • Week 2
© Houghton Mifflin Harcourt Publishing Company. All rights reserved.

Name _____

Vowel Team oo and vowel u /o͝o/

The vowel team *oo* and the vowel *u* can both stand for the /o͝o/ sound, as in *book* and *push*.

▶ Read the words. Circle the grapheme that stands for the /o͝o/ sound in each word. Then write the word that best describes each picture on the line.

1. hook   good
   cook   wool   _____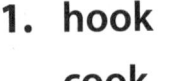

2. shook   hoof
   foot   soot   _____

3. cooking   bookshelf
   notebook   football   _____

4. push   bull
   pull   put   _____

5. hood   soot
   full   wood   _____

6. brook   stood
   look   crook   _____

Grade 2 — Module 9 • Week 2

Name _____

Read and Spell

Read and spell this word to be a better reader.

📖 Read it.

friend

👆 Tap the sounds.

○ ○ ○ ○ ○ ○ ○

✏️ Color it by sound.

friend

✏️ Write it.

_____

✏️ Write it again.

_____

📖 Read it.

"It looks like we are all set to bake the muffins for our friend," Brook said.
I have more than one best friend.

✏️ Write it in a sentence.

_____

_____

Irregular Words

Name _____

Decodable Text

A Perfect Day

Gran and I put the saddles on the horses. I gave the barn door a push with my foot. The old wood creaked.

Our dog Sooty woofed when he spied us.

"Okay, you can come with us this time," I said.

We took the path by the brook. We rode until we got to the crooked tree and then got off the horses. The branches shook in the breeze, and I pulled up my hood against the chill.

I looked at Gran. "I'm glad you said we should wear our wool coats."

I took out my hoof pick and checked our horses' feet. The hoof pick had a hook to clean out each hoof. Good, they had not picked up any rocks.

Gran and I sat below the tree with our books. We both love to relax and read there, away from the rest of the world.

"What a perfect day," I said.

Gran smiled over the top of the book in her hands. "I agree," she said.

▶ Draw a picture that shows what you read in the text.

Name _____

Decodable Text

Baking with Dad

Brook put on her apron and took out a cookbook.

She stood beside Dad at the oven.

"It looks like we are all set to bake the muffins for our friend," Brook said.

Dad pushed a bowl to Brook. "The first step is to mix this up," he said.

"I am good at mixing," Brook said.

Dad used his foot to pull a bench closer. "Stand on this so you can see. When you stood on the floor, you seemed low," Dad said.

"Thanks," Brook said. "I hope our muffins look as good as the ones on this page!"

Dad handed Brook a cup of raisins, and she shook them into the mix. Then, they put the mix into the cups of a muffin pan.

The last step was for Dad to put the pan into the oven and set the timer.

After the muffins sat for a bit, Dad and Brook could taste them. "They look and smell amazing," Brook said.

"And they taste even better!" Dad added in between bites.

▶ Draw a picture that shows what you read in the text.

Vocabulary

Name _____

Power Words: Draw and Write

Word Bank

attached   crack   surface   wraps

▶ Draw a picture or write words that will help you remember each Power Word from *Sea Otter Pups*. Try to write more than you draw.

1. attached

2. crack

3. surface

4. wraps

Name _____

Comprehension

Text Features

Authors may use different text features to organize information. This makes the information easier for the reader to find or understand. **Captions** give information about pictures. **Labels** name the parts of a picture. **Headings** tell what a page or section of a text is about. **Graphics** are visual features that include pictures, symbols, and **maps**.

▶ Answer the questions about *Sea Otter Pups*.

🔍 Page 187 What do the heading and labels on this page tell you?

_____

_____

_____

🔍 Page 188 Why are there two maps, and what is the purpose of the yellow highlighting?

_____

_____

_____

_____

_____

_____

Grade 2   252   Module 9 • Week 2

Name _____

Phonics Review

The vowel team *oo* and the vowel *u* can both stand for the /o͝o/ sound, as in *book* and *push*.

▶ Choose and write the word that answers the clue.

1. This can be in a chimney. _____

   foot   soot   put

2. An animal with horns. _____

   wool   full   bull

3. This is used to fish. _____

   hook   shook   took

4. A person does this in a kitchen. _____

   cook   bull   wood

5. This is something we read. _____

   bull   brook   book

6. A jacket might have one. _____

   hood   wood   good

Name _____

Generative Vocabulary

Prefix mis-

Add a **prefix** to the beginning of a **base word** to change its meaning. The prefix *mis-* means "wrong." Use a dictionary to find the meaning of base words that you do not know.

▶ Add the prefix *mis-* to each base word. Then write a sentence using the new word.

1. spell _____

_____

_____

2. use _____

_____

_____

_____

3. counted _____

_____

_____

_____

4. read _____

_____

_____

Vocabulary

Name _____

Power Words: Yes or No?

Word Bank

hide   sheltered   weary   wit

▶ Read each sentence. Circle **YES** if the word makes sense or **NO** if it does not. Rewrite the sentence so it makes sense.

1. A rabbit has a furry **hide**.

   YES   NO

_____

2. An open area is a **sheltered** place to wait during a storm.

   YES   NO

_____

_____

3. If you feel **weary**, you do not need to rest.

   YES   NO

_____

_____

4. A person with **wit** does not act funny.

   YES   NO

Name _____

Comprehension

Elements of Poetry

Poetry is a special kind of writing. The words in poems create pictures and make music. **Rhythm** gives the words in poems a beat. **Rhyme** happens when words end with the same sounds. **Repetition** is when the same words or lines appear over and over. Poets often use **descriptive language** to help readers picture what they are writing about.

▶ Answer the questions about *At Home in the Wild*.

🔍 Pages 202–203 What do you notice about which words rhyme in the first two stanzas? Why do you think the poet did this? Why do you think the poet used repeating lines in the poem?

_____

_____

_____

_____

🔍 Pages 204–206 Why do you think each verse begins with the same phrase? What do you notice about the second line in each verse?

_____

_____

_____

Name _____

Phonics

Vowel Teams: oo, ou /ū/

The vowel teams *oo* and *ou* can stand for the /ū/ sound, as in the words *goose* and *soup*.

▶ Read the question and look at the picture. Write the word that answers the question.

Can it **scoop** or **droop**?

_____

Is it a **group** or a **groom**?

_____

Is it a **zoo** or **soup**?

_____

Is it the **moon** or a **wound**?

_____

Is it a **toadstool** or **stepstool**?

_____

Does it have a **tooth** or a **roof**?

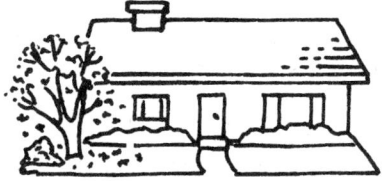

_____

Name _____

Phonics

Vowel Teams: oo, ou /ū/

You can spell the /ū/ sound with *oo*, as in *goose*, or *ou*, as in *soup*.

▶ Write the word from the word bank that best completes each sentence.

Word Bank

root
youth
spoon
bloom
wound
room
you
group
boost
scoop

1. Spring is the season when everything is in _____ .

2. My study _____ meets each week to help each other with homework.

3. Have _____ ever been in an airplane?

4. The oak tree has a huge _____ system!

5. It is best to eat soup with a _____ .

6. The nurse put a bandage on my small _____ .

7. I gave my baby sister a _____ to help her get on the chair.

8. I love to hear my grandpa tell stories about his _____ .

▶ Write a sentence with the word from the word bank you did not use.

_____

Grade 2
© Houghton Mifflin Harcourt Publishing Company. All rights reserved.
Module 9 • Week 3

Irregular Words

Name _____

Read and Spell

Read and spell this word to be a better reader.

📖 Read it.

move

👆 Tap the sounds.

○○○○○○○

✏️ Color it by sound.

move

✏️ Write it.

_____

✏️ Write it again.

_____

📖 Read it.

We will move into our home next week.

The clock hands move to show the time.

✏️ Write it in a sentence.

_____

_____

Grade 2 259 Module 9 • Week 3

Name _____

Irregular Words

Read and Spell

Read and spell this word to be a better reader.

📖 Read it.	👆 Tap the sounds.
prove	○○○○○○○

✏️ Color it by sound.

prove

✏️ Write it.	✏️ Write it again.
_____	_____

📖 Read it.

But the goose zoomed to the roof as if to prove she does not want her food.
Facts are things you can prove to be correct.

✏️ Write it in a sentence.

_____

_____

Grade 2 259a Module 9 • Week 3
© Houghton Mifflin Harcourt Publishing Company. All rights reserved.

Decodable Text

Name _____

Group Trip

Boone's school group went on a trip. They visited an old home called a manor. Everything in it was from a long time ago.

A woman in a wide hoop skirt met them at the door. "Welcome," she said. "My name is Ruth. I will show you around the manor."

Ruth led the group from room to room.

The "great room" had a long table that could seat at least fourteen people. The kitchen in the next room had huge stoves and a rack with hanging pots and pans that you can move.

One small room upstairs had a loom to weave fabric. Ruth showed the group what to do to work the loom.

Then, after the group toured the rest of the rooms, Ruth led them outside. "We have a coop for chickens and a rooster," she said. "Can you make out anything more?"

"There is a goose, too," Boone said.

At noon, the class had soup for lunch. They scooped it up with wooden spoons. Then they packed up their things and trooped back to school.

▶ Draw a picture that shows what you read in the text.

Decodable Text

Name _____

Goose on the Loose

LouAnn sipped her soup.

"Woof!" Her pooch looked out the window as something waddled into their garden.

"Mom," LouAnn said, "Cooper's goose is loose again!"

Mom and LouAnn dashed outside. "Shoo!" Mom said. "There is no food here for you. You need to go home to your pool."

Soon, Cooper ran up.

"Why does your goose choose our garden?" LouAnn asked.

"When the moon is full, she gets in a mood," Cooper said. "She does not want her regular food. She likes the blooms and roots in your garden. I will take her home."

But the goose zoomed to the roof as if to prove she does not want her food.

"Can you boost me up?" Cooper asked.

"No," Mom said. "That is not safe."

"We need a hot air balloon," LouAnn said. "Then we could fly to the roof."

"She will come back soon," Mom said. "Then Cooper can take her home and build a better goose coop."

▶ Draw a picture that shows what you read in the text.

Name _____

Vocabulary

Power Words: Match

Word Bank

| arrive | growled | grumpy | joking |
| offered | shrugged | stubborn | tucked |

▶ Write the Power Word from *Abuelo and the Three Bears* that best fits each item.

1. When you say something to be funny, you are doing this. _____

2. This word describes someone who is in a bad mood. _____

3. Which word means *reach* or *come to*? _____

4. When someone does not want to change, they are this. _____

5. This is what you did when you asked a friend if you could help. _____

6. If a dog did this, you would want to stay away. _____

7. Which word means *pushed behind or into*? _____

8. When I didn't know the answer to my friend's question, I did this. _____

Grade 2

Module 9 • Week 3

© Houghton Mifflin Harcourt Publishing Company. All rights reserved.

Name _____

Comprehension

Figurative Language

Literal language means just what it says. **Figurative language** uses words in different ways. It makes writing colorful and interesting. An **idiom** is a phrase that means something different from its everyday meaning. A **hyperbole** is a statement that is so crazy it can't be true.

▶ Answer the questions about *Abuelo and the Three Bears*.

🔍 Page 217 If you are so hungry that you could eat an elephant, how hungry are you? Why does the author use hyperbole?

_____
_____
_____
_____

🔍 Page 220 Abuelo says that Trencitas "followed her nose." What does this idiom mean? Explain why the idiom has this meaning.

_____
_____
_____
_____
_____
_____

Name _____

Phonics

Phonics Review

The vowel team *oo* can stand for the vowel sound you hear in the word *goose*. The vowel team *ou* can stand for the vowel sound you hear in the word *soup*.

▶ Choose and write two words to complete each sentence.

1. Lou took a _____ on a trip to the _____ .

   zoo   tooth   wound   group

2. It was a _____ day, so the group hoped the animals would be in a good _____ .

   goose   mood   cool   you

3. At the bird exhibit, they watched _____ dip and _____ in the air.

   loop   toucans   youth   broom

4. The group also watched a huge _____ swim in a big _____ .

   pool   soup   goose   too

5. Then, they watched the zookeeper give a _____ of _____ to each bird.

   wound   scoop   roof   food

Name _____

Generative Vocabulary

Prefix pre-

Add a **prefix** in front of a **base word** to change the meaning of the word. The prefix *pre–* means "before." If you do not know the meaning of a base word, look the word up in a dictionary.

▶ Add the prefix *pre–* to each word. Then write the meaning of the new word.

1. sliced: _____

2. cook: _____

3. paid: _____

4. measure: _____

5. package: _____

▶ Choose two words with the prefix *pre–* from above and write a sentence for each. Check the meaning of base words you do not know in a dictionary.

6. _____
   _____.

7. _____
   _____.

Grade 2
© Houghton Mifflin Harcourt Publishing Company. All rights reserved.

Vowel Teams: ew, ui, ue /ū/

You can spell the /ū/ sound with the vowel teams *ew*, *ui*, and *ue* as in *screw*, *juice*, and *glue*.

▶ Read the question and look at the picture. Write the word that answers the question.

Does it **cruise** or **bruise**?

_____

Is it a **suitcase** or a **stewpot**?

_____

Is it **glue** or **dew**?

_____

Is it a **blueprint** or a **bluebird**?

_____

Is it a **screw** or a **fruit**?

_____

Is it **juice** or a **crew**?

_____

Phonics

Name _____

Vowel Teams: ew, ui, ue /ū/

You can spell the /ū/ sound with the vowel teams *ew*, *ui*, and *ue* as in *screw*, *juice*, and *glue*.

▶ Read each clue. Unscramble the tiles. Write the word from the word bank correctly on the line.

Word Bank

new crew glue fruit grew blue juice stew true cruise

1. You can drink this. [ui] [j] [ce] _____

2. This is a thick soup. [t] [ew] [s] _____

3. Not old [ew] [n] _____

4. A type of big ship [se] [r] [c] [ui] _____

5. Sticks things together [ue] [l] [g] _____

6. Some kinds grow on trees. [t] [ui] [f] [r] _____

7. A group of people [r] [c] [ew] _____

8. The sky is this shade. [ue] [l] [b] _____

9. Not false [r] [t] [ue] _____

Grade 2   Module 10 • Week 1

Name _____

Phonics Review

The vowel teams *ew, ui,* and *ue* can stand for the /ū/ sound, as in *screw, juice,* and *glue.*

▶ Choose and write two words to complete each sentence.

1. I packed my _____ for my first trip on a

   _____ ship!

   fruit **cruise** **juicebox** **suitcase**

2. I got a brand _____ _____ to wear

   in the pool.

   swimsuit **new** **glue** **dew**

3. On the day of the cruise, the sky was a cool

   _____ and the wind _____ softly.

   screw **blue** **juice** **blew**

4. On the ship, the _____ showed us the

   safety boats in case of a _____ emergency.

   crew **bruise** **true** **grew**

5. Then, I was able to get some fresh _____

   _____ and hang by the pool!

   clue **juice** **flew** **fruit**

Name _____

Irregular Words

Read and Spell

Read and spell this word to be a better reader.

📖 Read it.

often

👆 Tap the sounds.

○ ○ ○ ○ ○ ○ ○

✏️ Color it by sound.

often

✏️ Write it.

✏️ Write it again.

📖 Read it.

Often on the cruise, we ate fresh fruit and other tasty foods, such as beef stew.
My family often goes to the pool to swim.

✏️ Write it in a sentence.

_____
_____

Irregular Words

Name _____

Read and Spell

Read and spell this word to be a better reader.

Read it.

listen

Tap the sounds.

○ ○ ○ ○ ○ ○ ○

Color it by sound.

listen

Write it.

_____

Write it again.

_____

Read it.

"But listen, X marks the spot with the loot," Lewis argued.
It is polite to listen carefully.

Write it in a sentence.

_____

_____

Grade 2   268a   Module 10 • Week 1
© Houghton Mifflin Harcourt Publishing Company. All rights reserved.

Name _____

Decodable Text

A Cruise Story

One day in art class, Sue drew a cruise ship. Then she told her friend Newt a story about it.

"My older sister and I went on this cruise ship for five days. When we first got on the ship, we spotted crew people in new blue suits. One of the crew members gave us a tour of the ship and showed us to our room.

Often on the cruise, we ate fresh fruit and other tasty foods, such as beef stew.

Then, one night, the air grew stormy. A cruel wind blew and blew, rocking the ship from side to side.

One of the crew slipped and fell. Then he rolled to the side of the ship!

'We have to help him,' my sister said.

I called to a woman close by, and she threw the man a rope to pull him back. He was safe!"

"What an exciting story," Newt said. "Is it true?"

"No," Sue said. "I just made it up to go with this ship I drew. But I'm glad you thought it was exciting. I'm going to enter it into a story contest!"

▶ Draw a picture that shows what you read in the text.

Name _____

Decodable Text

Clues to the Loot

When Lewis and his mom moved into their new home, he came across an old paper.

"Look, Mom!" Lewis said. "It is a map with clues. I think a pioneer crew drew it!"

Mom was using glue to fix a vase that had broken during the move. "I do not know if that is true," Mom said.

"But listen, X marks the spot with the loot," Lewis argued.

Mom scanned the map. "Some of the clues look like our backyard."

"You are right," Lewis said. "I will follow the clues, find the X spot, and dig there."

"Please finish your snack and juice first," Mom said. "Then you can look."

Lewis chugged his juice. Then he threw on a coat and flew outside. He knew he could find the loot. He followed the clues to the X and started digging. But he did not find any loot.

"That is a shame," Mom said. "But at least that hole will suit my new rosebush."

▶ Draw a picture that shows what you read in the text.

Grade 2 • Vowel Teams *ew, ui, ue* /ū/   269a   Module 10 • Week 1

Name _____

Vocabulary

Power Words: Match

Word Bank

| darting | delight | fragrant | grunted |
| hollered | nod | slippery | smothered |

▶ Write the Power Word from *Where on Earth Is My Bagel?* that best fits each item.

1. When the bear made a low, deep sound, it did this. _____

2. This movement of your head means you agree. _____

3. Which word means *great joy*? _____

4. This word means the same as *shouted loudly*. _____

5. This is how something that is smooth and wet feels. _____

6. Which word means *moving quickly from place to place*? _____

7. What is it called when food is thickly covered in a sauce? _____

8. Which word means the opposite of *stinky*? _____

Name _____

Suffixes –ion, –tion, –sion

A **suffix** is a word part added to the end of a **base word**. It changes the meaning of the word. The suffixes *–ion*, *–tion*, and *–sion* mean "an act of," "a condition of," or "the result of." Use a dictionary to look up the meaning of base words you do not know.

Word Bank

| celebration | confusion | hibernation |
| instruction | prediction | separation |

▶ Choose the word from the box that best matches each definition. Write the word on the line.

1. the act of celebrating something _____

2. the act of predicting the future _____

3. the condition of not understanding _____

4. the condition of hibernating _____

5. the act of instructing _____

6. the result of separating _____

Name _____

Comprehension

Theme

The **theme** of a story is the big idea, **moral**, or lesson the author wants readers to take away. To find the theme, identify the **topic**, or what the story is mostly about. Next look for evidence to figure out the message the author wants you to learn. Say the theme in your own words.

▶ Answer the questions about *Where on Earth Is My Bagel?*

🔍 Pages 247–251 Who is the story's main character, and what problem does he have? How does Yum Yung try to solve his problem?

_____

_____

_____

_____

_____

🔍 Pages 260–264 What does Yum Yung realize about where he can get a bagel? Use evidence from the text to explain your answer. What theme, or big idea, does this help you figure out?

_____

_____

_____

_____

Name _____

Vocabulary Strategy

Shades of Meaning

Shades of meaning are the small differences in meaning between words that are **synonyms**, or mean the same thing.

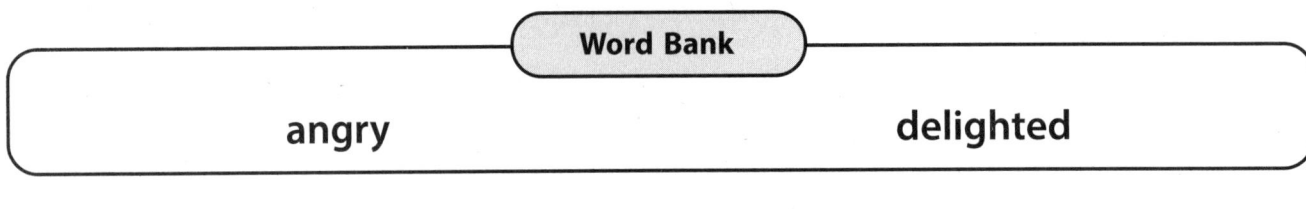

Word Bank

angry   delighted

▶ Fill in each blank with a synonym from the box.

1. (least) _____ (greatest)

    happy   pleased   _____

2. (least) _____ (greatest)

    upset   _____   furious

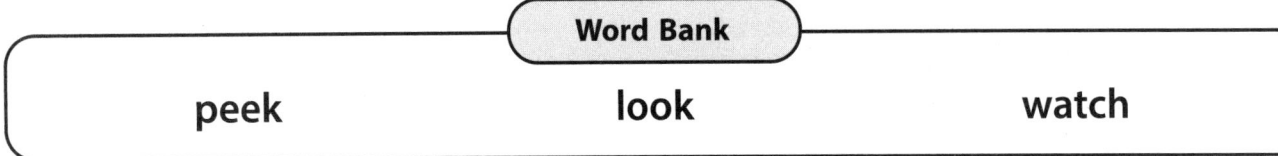

Word Bank

peek   look   watch

▶ Put the words in order, from least to greatest. Then complete each sentence.

_____

3. I _____ at my teacher when she is talking.

4. Cover your eyes, and don't _____ !

5. We will _____ the movie together.

Name _____

Research

Follow a Research Plan

A research plan is a list of steps to follow to do a research project. Follow these steps:

1. Select a topic.
2. Ask questions about the topic.
3. Pick resources to use for your research.
4. Keep a record of the resources you use to avoid **plagiarism**, or copying another person's work without giving credit.
5. Organize the information.
6. Decide how you want to share the information.
7. Present the information.

Research Prompt: Think about something from *Where on Earth Is My Bagel?* that you would like to know more about. Create a research plan that will help you complete your research project.

1. Write your topic: I would like to learn more about _____.

2. Write three research questions about the topic. What do you want to know?

   1. _____

   2. _____

   3. _____

Name _____

Research

3. Pick your sources. Look for answers to your research questions. Write the information you find in your sources.

_____

_____

_____

4. Keep a record of the resources you use. Write the titles and names of authors in the chart.

Record of My Sources	
Title	Author's Name

5. Organize the information you found. Tell what you learned.

1. _____

2. _____

3. _____

6. How will you share your information? Circle one or two.

writing   drawing   talking

Name _____

Phonics

Vowel Teams au, aw, ough

The vowel teams *au*, *aw*, and *ough* can stand for the /aw/ sound, as in the words *pause*, *saw*, and *bought*.

▶ Write the word that names the picture. Circle the grapheme that stands for the /aw/ sound.

1. stall   straw   sought

   _____

2. lawful   lawn   launch

   _____

3. dot   drawing   dawn

   _____

4. faucet   fawn   fought

   _____

5. bawling   bought   baseball

   _____

6. seesaw   sawdust   sawhorse

   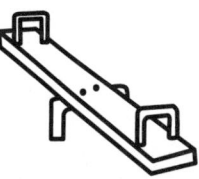

   _____

Name _____

Phonics

Vowel Teams au, aw, ough

The vowel teams *au*, *aw*, and *ough* can stand for the /aw/ sound, as in the words *pause*, *saw*, and *bought*.

Word Bank

brought
draw
gauze
pause
bought
lawn
thought
paw
launch

▶ Write the word that best completes each sentence.

1. I had to _____ the song so I could hear my mom.

2. My dog hurt his _____ .

3. I _____ my pet rock for show and tell.

4. I like to help my mom mow the _____ .

5. I love to _____ bugs in my sketch book.

6. My family went to watch the space _____ .

7. He _____ it was a good plan.

8. The nurse put some _____ on my arm.

▶ Write a sentence with the word from the word bank you did not use.

_____

_____

_____

Irregular Words

Name _____

Read and Spell

Read and spell this word to be a better reader.

Read it.
laugh

Tap the sounds.
○○○○○○○

Color it by sound.
laugh

Write it.
_____

Write it again.
_____

Read it.

The joke made me laugh!

I can hear his laugh from the next room.

Write it in a sentence.

_____

_____

Grade 2   278   Module 10 • Week 2

Name _____

Decodable Text

Paul's Good Plan

My big brother Paul had a plan to get up at dawn to see the space launch.

I was asleep when a paw landed on my face. I let out a squawk. It was my dog, Fawn. Fawn wanted me to wake up so we could go outside with Paul.

I crawled out of bed and fought off a yawn. I wrapped up in a shawl and followed Paul and Fawn outside.

Paul brought a quilt. I grabbed one side and we laid it on the lawn so we could sprawl on our backs. Fawn lay beside me to keep me cozy. But the chilly air caused me to cough. I thought I should go back inside, but I paused when I saw a light rise into the sky.

"There is the launch," Paul said.

I watched in awe as the spaceship left Earth. It was just like our teacher told us in class.

"This was a good plan, Paul!"

▶ Draw a picture that shows what you read in the text.

Name _____

Decodable Text

Why Do We Yawn?

If you saw someone yawn, it might have caused you to yawn. If you read about a yawn or saw an image of one, it could have caused you to yawn, even if you fought not to. Don't laugh! You may have even yawned just now while reading this text.

We yawn a lot, about five to twenty times a day. Some experts say humans' yawns last about six seconds. When you yawn, your jaws open wide and you take in more air.

People yawn the most when they first wake up. A yawn may also happen when you are tired or sleepy.

A dog may yawn when it is stressed or worried. Some animals, such as hippos and baboons, yawn as a clue they might fight. Even fish yawn. One study showed that animals with bigger brains yawn longer.

There is no proven cause for why we yawn. It is thought to be a way to cool an overheated brain. It could be a way to stay alert. But we may never know exactly why.

▶ Draw a picture that shows what you read in the text.

Vocabulary

Power Words: Yes or No?

Word Bank

clutched   forgot   races   trunk

▶ Read each sentence. Circle **YES** if the word makes sense or **NO** if it does not. Rewrite the sentence so it makes sense.

1. A squirrel is an animal that **races** up and down the **trunk** of a tree.

   YES   NO

   _____

2. Meg **clutched** her friend's arm so that she could fall down.

   YES   NO

   _____

   _____

3. Peter came to the party because Rachel **forgot** to invite him.

   YES   NO

   _____

   _____

Name _____

Comprehension

Central Idea

The **topic** of a text is the person or thing that text is mostly about. The **central idea** is the most important idea about the topic. Readers can use **supporting evidence**, or details, facts, and examples, to figure out the central idea.

▶ Answer the questions about *May Day Around the World*.

🔍 Pages 270–271 What is this text mostly about? How do you know?

_____
_____
_____

🔍 Pages 272–274 What details in this part of the text give more information about May Day celebrations? What central idea do these details support?

_____
_____
_____
_____
_____
_____

Name _____

Phonics

Phonics Review

The vowel teams *au, aw,* and *ough* can stand for the /aw/ sound, as in the words *pause, saw,* and *bought.*

▶ Choose and write two words to complete each sentence.

1. I watched as the _____ _____ to keep up with their mom.

   brought   fawns   fought   saw

2. The _____ gave me his _____ .

   also   author   awfully   autograph

3. After raking the _____, I had to _____ the leaves away.

   caused   haul   brought   lawn

4. I _____ the artist's _____ at the fair.

   drawing   seesaw   sawing   bought

5. My new tooth _____ my _____ to feel sore.

   ought   jaw   paused   caused

6. The nurse _____ _____ in her first aid kit.

   brought   yawn   sprawl   gauze

Name _____

Suffixes –y, –ly

Add a **suffix** to the end of a **base word** to change its meaning. The suffix –y means, "having or being like something." The suffix –ly explains how or when something is done.

▶ Add –y or –ly to the base word to make a new word. Write the new word and its meaning on the line.

1. snow + y = _____ : _____

2. quick + ly = _____ : _____

3. dirt + y _____ : _____

Definition Bank

| in a silly or foolish way | in a confident way |
| being cold | having a lot of grease |

▶ Choose the definition from the box that matches each word. Write it on the line. Circle *adjective* if the word is a describing word. Circle *adverb* if the word tells how or when.

4. chilly: _____   adjective   adverb

5. foolishly: _____   adjective   adverb

6. greasy: _____   adjective   adverb

7. confidently: _____   adjective   adverb

Name _____

Vocabulary

Power Words: Draw and Write

Word Bank

final   founded   imaginary   patient

▶ Draw a picture or write words that will help you remember each Power Word from *Goal!* Try to write more than you draw.

1. final

2. founded

3. imaginary

4. patient

Name _____

Comprehension

Central Idea

The **topic** of a text is the person or thing that text is mostly about. The **central idea** is the most important idea about the topic. You can figure out the central idea by looking for **supporting evidence**—details, facts, or examples in the text—that tells about the central idea.

▶ Answer the questions about *Goal!*

🔍 Pages 280–281 What is the topic of this text? What evidence helps you identify the topic? What do details in this part of the text help you understand about the topic?

_____

_____

_____

🔍 Pages 286–288 What important idea about soccer does the author share with readers? What supporting evidence helps you understand the central idea?

_____

_____

_____

_____

Name _____

Vowel Team ea /ĕ/

We know that the vowel team *ea* can stand for the /ē/ sound, as in *team*. This vowel team can also stand for the short *e* sound, /ĕ/, as in *bread*.

▶ Write the word that names the picture. Circle the grapheme that stands for the short *e* sound.

bed belly bread	feather breakfast weather

_____	_____
stead spread head	health breath wealth

_____	_____
threat thread three	sweater meadow bedspread

_____	_____

Name _____

Phonics

Vowel a: /ŏ/

We already know that the vowel *a* can stand for the sound /ă/, as in *apple*, and /ā/, as in *acorn*. Sometimes, *a* can also stand for the /ŏ/ sound, as in *wash*. Vowel *a* usually stands for /ŏ/ when it follows consonant *w* or the letter combination *qu*, as in *quad*.

▶ Write the word that names the picture. Circle the grapheme that stands for the /ŏ/ sound.

1. wash   waste   wand
    _____

2. swamp   swan   squat
    _____

3. wad   want   watch
    _____

4. walrus   wander   waddle
    _____

5. wasp   wallet   wallow
    _____

Grade 2   287   Module 10 • Week 3
© Houghton Mifflin Harcourt Publishing Company. All rights reserved.

Name _____

Irregular Words

Read and Spell

Read and spell this word to be a better reader.

📖 Read it.

through

👆 Tap the sounds.

○ ○ ○ ○ ○ ○ ○

✏️ Color it by sound.

through

✏️ Write it.

_____

✏️ Write it again.

_____

📖 Read it.

Aunt Lue and Billy hike through the trees and up a big hill.
A little mouse ran through the hole in the wall.

✏️ Write it in a sentence.

_____

_____

Grade 2   288   Module 10 • Week 3

Name _____

Decodable Text

At the Park

"It is going to be very hot," Aunt Lue said. "But I read there is no threat of rain today."

"Can we still go to the park?" Billy asked.

"Yes, go get dressed," Aunt Lue said.

Aunt Lue got out bread and made sandwiches. She packed them with fruit and cold drinks.

The park was close, and they got there in no time. Aunt Lue spread out a blanket.

It was not time for lunch yet, so Aunt Lue and Billy hiked through the trees and up a big hill to play catch. Then they raced to the swings to see who could go the highest.

"You got it right about it being hot today, Aunt Lue," Billy said, patting the sweat off his face.

"Well, at least it's not raining," Aunt Lue said. "We can sit in the shade and eat."

Billy took one bite of his sandwich and felt something drip on his head. "My, my," he said. "I think it might rain after all."

"It's okay," Aunt Lue said. "It's just sprinkling. And it feels good in this heat!"

▶ Draw a picture that shows what you read in the text.

Name _____

Decodable Text

Swans

"Hi, Cam. What are you up to?" Uncle Zev asked.

"I am reading about swans. We are studying them in class," Cam said.

"Would you like to swap that book for some real swans?" Uncle Zev said. "There is a swamp in back of the barn. There may be some swans there today."

"Yes!" Cam said.

She checked with Mom and then sprinted to Uncle Zev's truck.

"Just watch where you sit," Uncle Zev said. "I do not want you to squash that bag."

Uncle Zev drove to the swamp. He spread out a blanket, and they sat and watched for the swans.

Then there was a splash.

Cam spotted the swan first. It was white with a long, curved neck and damp wings.

The swan came on the land. "Look at its webbed feet. I bet they help it swim fast," Cam said.

Then Cam watched the swan run and lift off. "Whoa, I've never seen a swan fly," Cam said.

"Yes, they are some of the largest flying birds in the world!" Uncle Zev said. "I'm glad you got to see the words from your book come to life."

▶ Draw a picture that shows what you read in the text.

Grade 2 • Vowel *a* /ŏ/

Name _____

Vocabulary

Power Words: Match

Word Bank

adventures   breathless   clamber   flitting
leave   mound   shuffled stacked

▶ Write the Power Word from *Poems in the Attic* that best fits each item.

1. This is how you walked when you dragged your feet. _____

2. How would you feel right after you ran many laps? _____

3. Which word describes a place that is filled up with something? _____

4. This is time away from work. _____

5. Which word has the same meaning as *hill* or *pile*? _____

6. This is how you are moving when you climb quickly. _____

7. Which word describes how a bird or butterfly is moving? _____

8. These are exciting experiences. _____

Name _____

Comprehension

Story Structure

Most stories have the same **story structure.** The **conflict,** or problem, the characters face is introduced in the beginning. In the middle of the story, **events** happen as characters try to solve the conflict. At the end of the story, events explain the **resolution,** or how the conflict is solved. The conflict, events, and resolution make up the story's **plot.**

▶ Answer the questions about *Poems in the Attic.*

🔍 Pages 294–301 What events happen in the beginning of the story? Use details from the poems to help you. What challenge does the girl face now that Mama once faced, too?

_____

_____

_____

_____

_____

🔍 Pages 308–310 How do the girl's story and Mama's story end? Use evidence to explain how each had their conflict resolved.

_____

_____

_____

_____

Name _____

Phonics Review

The vowel team *ea* can stand for the /ĕ/ sound, as in *bread*.

The vowel *a* can stand for the /ŏ/ sound, as in *wash*. Vowel *a* usually stands for /ŏ/ when it follows consonant *w* or letter combination *qu*.

Word Bank

wash
swamp
thread
health
want
watch
weather
wander

▶ Write the word that best completes each sentence.

1. We took a boat ride through the _____ .

2. I like to _____ through the park on sunny days.

3. Eating the right food is good for your _____ .

4. The _____ today is cold and rainy.

5. You should _____ your hands.

6. He used a needle and _____ to stitch the button back on.

7. We went to _____ the show at the park.

▶ Write a sentence with the word from the word bank you did not use.

_____

Name _____

Generative Vocabulary

Suffixes –ion, –tion, –sion

A **suffix** is a word part added to the end of a base word that changes the meaning of the word. The suffixes *–ion*, *–tion*, and *–sion* mean "an act of," "a condition of," or "the result of."

▶ Write the meaning of each base word. Use the base word and suffix to determine the meaning of each new word. Look up base words you do not know in a dictionary.

Base Word and Meaning	Suffix	New Word	Meaning
1. illustrate _____	–ion	illustration	
2. expand _____	–sion	expansion	
3. reproduce _____	–tion	reproduction	

▶ Underline the suffix, and write the meaning of the new word on the line. You may use a dictionary to look up the base word.

1. election: _____

Grade 2   293   Module 10 • Week 3

Name _____

VC/CV Syllable Division Pattern

When a word has two consonants between two vowels, the Rabbit Rule tells us to divide between the consonants (*rab-bit*). When we see three consonants between two vowels, remember to keep blends and digraphs together.

▶ Read each word. Draw a line (/) to divide each word into syllables.

breakfast	walrus	toothpaste
laundry	bookshelf	swimsuit

▶ Use the words above to complete the sentences.

1. We saw a _____ at the sea-life exhibit at the zoo.

2. My sister and I help fold the _____ each week.

3. I almost have too many books for my _____ !

4. I put the cap back on my tube of _____ .

▶ Write a sentence for each of the words you did not use.

5. _____
   _____

6. _____
   _____

V/CV and VC/V Syllable Division Patterns

When a word has one consonant between two vowels, the Tiger Rule tells us to divide after the first vowel (*ti-ger*).

When a word has one consonant between two vowels and the Tiger Rule does not work, the Camel Rule tells us to divide after the consonant (*cam-el*).

When dividing a word into syllables, vowel teams, digraphs, and blends stay together.

▶ Draw a line (/) to divide each word into syllables.

cozy	twilight	cashews
hotel	menu	second

▶ Use the words above to complete the sentences.

1. I like to put _____ in my trail mix.

2. The family stayed in a _____ with a pool.

3. I love reading my book in the _____ nook.

4. What will you order from the _____ ?

5. The lake looks beautiful in the _____ .

6. I took a _____ to rest my legs.

Name _____

Phonics

Syllable Division Review

When a word has two consonants between two vowels, the Rabbit Rule tells us to divide between the consonants (*rab-bit*).

When a word has one consonant between two vowels, the Tiger Rule tells us to divide after the first vowel (*ti-ger*).

When a word has one consonant between two vowels and the Tiger Rule does not work, the Camel Rule tells us to divide after the consonant (*cam-el*).

▶ Draw a line (/) to divide each word into syllables. Then write each word in the correct column.

Word Bank

cactus   body   music   rainbow   finish   tulip
dragon   helmet   moment   begin   solid   trumpet

Rabbit Rule	**Tiger Rule**	**Camel Rule**
_____	_____	_____
_____	_____	_____
_____	_____	_____
_____	_____	_____

Grade 2   296   Module 11 • Week 1

Decodable Text

Name _____

My Poodle Puppies

My poodle gave birth to a litter of puppies last month. The tiny newborn puppies ate, yawned, and sprawled beside their mother.

Then, before I knew it, the puppies outgrew their box and started causing trouble. If I turned my back, they headed through the hall on unsteady paws. I had to help them because they were clueless about the dangers. I did not want them to try scooting toward the stairs!

Sometimes they were a nuisance, pawing and chewing on anything they could find. One sly puppy tried crawling under their new gate and almost got stuck. And one saucy pup went cruising into my sister's room, but I scooped him up just in time.

After that, I asked my family to be thoughtful and get into the habit of closing their doors instead of leaving them open. If they did not, they might find a puppy chewing on their best sweater. No one argued with me, not even my sister.

Soon, the puppies will be ready to go to their new homes, and despite their troublemaking, I will miss them.

▶ Draw a picture that shows what you read in the text.

Name _____

Decodable Text

Game Day

Scooter woke up not long after the day was dawning. Today was the day Scooter and Mom would go to the football game! It was the Cougars against the Cruisers.

He pulled on the maroon team shirt that his big brother outgrew. It was too large, but he loved it. He pulled his cap over his crewcut. He was ready!

He ran to the table. It was still early, but he wanted Mom to know he was not a sleepyhead.

Mom had made waffles with fruit for them, and she was looking at the weather forecast.

"Awful news," Mom said. "The clouds are threatening to rain."

Scooter watched the newscast. It said a storm was brewing. Scooter still wanted to go to the game. But Mom said no because Scooter had been coughing. It would not be wise for Scooter to be in the rain.

Scooter did not argue, because Mom had a plan.

"I have a coupon for chicken wings. We'll eat wings and watch the game on the screen instead."

▶ Draw a picture that shows what you read in the text.

Name _____

Phonics

Vowel Team Diphthongs ou, ow

The vowel teams *ou* and *ow* can stand for the same sound, /ow/. They can stand for the vowel sound you hear in the words *house* and *cow*.

▶ Choose and write two words to complete each sentence.

1. A _____ saw a spark on the _____ .

       mount   **mouse**   **loud**   **ground**

2. It ran _____ the forest _____ the alarm.

       around   **account**   **slouching**   **sounding**

3. A _____ of animals started to _____ .

       spouts   **crown**   **crowd**   **shout**

4. "Stand back _____ !" Bear _____ .

       now   **noun**   **growled**   **grouch**

5. Bear _____ the flame with a _____ .

       scouted   **shower**   **down**   **drowned**

6. The animals clapped _____ when the flame was _____ .

       out   **owl**   **loudly**   **lousy**

Name _____

Vowel Team Diphthongs oi, oy

Phonics

The vowel teams *oi* and *oy* can stand for the same sound, /oi/. They can stand for the vowel sound you hear in the words *coin* and *toy*.

▶ Read each clue. Write the word from the word bank that best answers each clue.

Word Bank

choice
coins
voice
coil
noisy
joyful
moist
cowboy
join
toys

1. I might work on a ranch. _____

2. You use them to buy things. _____

3. We play with these. _____

4. If you decide something, _____
   you make this.

5. This means very happy. _____

6. You use this to speak. _____

7. This means wet or damp. _____

8. It looks like a twist or spiral. _____

9. This means very loud. _____

▶ Write a sentence with the word from the word bank that you did not use.

_____

_____

Name _____

Phonics Review

- The vowel team diphthongs *ou* and *ow* can stand for the vowel sound in *house* and *cow*. The vowel team diphthongs *oi* and *oy* can stand for the vowel sound in *coin* and *toy*.

▶ Read the clues. Write the word that answers the clue.

1. I am a name for a light rain.

    shower   shouter   scouting   

2. I tell how a happy child feels.

    jointed   joyful   jousting   

3. I am a name for pants.

    towel   toilet   trousers   

4. I am what you might say if your soup is too hot.

    Couch!   Ouch!   Oil!   _____

5. I mean that a food is rotten.

    soybeans   sprouting   spoiled   

6. I have petals and can grow in the ground.

    flounder   fountain   flower   

Name _____

Decodable Text

Owls

Look up. You may see some birds fly past the clouds, but you are not likely to see owls. That is because owls fly at night.

During the day, most owls can be found nesting in holes in trees. Some owls nest on the ground.

Most owls have soft brown, gray, or white feathers, with bars, streaks, or spots. This helps owls hide in the trees. Some owls have feathers that look like horns that stick out on the crown of their heads.

An owl has a flat face. Its beak and claws are sharp. An owl can turn its head around. An owl can spot prey, such as a mouse, far down below.

Owls make loud hoots, but that is not the only sound they make. When they fly, their wings can sound like a clap. An owl may also sing with chirps. So, when you are out at night, stay alert, and you might just find an owl.

▶ Draw a picture that shows what you read in the text.

Name _____

Decodable Text

Roy's Toy Store

My dad's name is Roy, and he makes toys. He has a shop called Roy's Toy Store. He sells lots of different toys.

One of the toys is a bank. It is shaped like a pig, and it talks each time you put in a coin. No, it doesn't say "Oink." It says things such as "Thank you" or "Feed me again."

Another toy is a boy with a dog on a leash. You can move one of the boy's arms to point and wave. The boy's other hand holds the dog's leash. And the dog can wag its tail.

The toy I like best is a little bird. You can wind it up and it makes a noise. I will not spoil the surprise, but maybe you know what kind of noise a little bird makes.

The toy Dad likes best is a girl he made to look like me. In a sweet voice, the girl sings a song my mom and dad sing to me at bedtime.

Dad says it gives him joy when someone loves one of his toys. So I hope you will come and find one of Dad's toys to love.

▶ Draw a picture that shows what you read in the text.

Name _____

V/V Syllable Division Pattern

When a word has two vowels together that don't make a vowel team, the Lion Rule tells us to divide between the vowels (*li-on*).

▶ Read each word, and then draw a line (/) to divide each word into syllables. Then write the word that best completes each sentence on the line.

1. **giant   client**

   I love the book about a bean and a _____!

2. **create   react**

   We helped Leo _____ a plan for the garden.

3. **neon   poem**

   I read the _____ out loud to my class.

4. **lion   riot**

   The lazy _____ slept under the tree.

5. **ruin   quiet**

   We must be _____ while we take the test.

6. **duet   dial**

   We sang a _____ for the talent show.

Name _____

Phonics

Syllable Division Review

We can use several rules to help us divide words into syllables:

- Rabbit Rule: Divide between the consonants (*rab-bit*).
- Tiger Rule: Divide after the first vowel (*ti-ger*).
- Camel Rule: Divide after the consonant that follows the first vowel (*cam-el*).
- Lion Rule: Divide between the vowels (*li-on*).

▶ Draw a line (/) to divide each word into syllables. Then write each word in the correct section.

Word Bank

napkin giant bacon planet triumph elbow
robin dentist raven wagon minus fluid

Rabbit Rule

_____

_____

_____

Tiger Rule

_____

_____

_____

Camel Rule

_____

_____

_____

Lion Rule

_____

_____

_____

Name _____

Phonics

Syllable Division Review

We can use several rules to help us divide words into syllables:

- Rabbit Rule: Divide between the consonants (*rab-bit*).
- Tiger Rule: Divide after the first vowel (*ti-ger*).
- Camel Rule: Divide after the consonant that follows the first vowel (*cam-el*).
- Lion Rule: Divide between the vowels (*li-on*).

▶ Draw a line (/) to divide each word into syllables. Then write the word that completes each sentence on the line.

1. **trial   tennis   toxic   total**
   I like to play _____ with my family on the weekends.

2. **pilot   planet   pillow   poem**
   I read my _____ out loud to the class for show and tell.

3. **fabric   frozen   fluid   finish**
   We skated across the _____ lake.

4. **robin   robot   riot   ribbon**
   The _____ flew from the nest and up into the sky.

5. **dial   dentist   demand   dragon**
   I can _____ my mom's number on the phone.

6. **magnet   meow   music   melon**
   What kind of _____ do you like to listen to?

Irregular Words

Name _____

Read and Spell

Read and spell this word to be a better reader.

📖 Read it.

honor

👆 Tap the sounds.

○ ○ ○ ○ ○ ○ ○

✏️ Color it by sound.

honor

✏️ Write it.

_____

✏️ Write it again.

_____

📖 Read it.
Some campgrounds give discounts to honor repeat campers.
It is an honor to meet you.

✏️ Write it in a sentence.

_____

_____

Grade 2   307   Module 11 • Week 3

© Houghton Mifflin Harcourt Publishing Company. All rights reserved.

Irregular Words

Name _____

Read and Spell

Read and spell this word to be a better reader.

📖 Read it.

honest

👆 Tap the sounds.

○ ○ ○ ○ ○ ○ ○

✏️ Color it by sound.

honest

✏️ Write it.

✏️ Write it again.

📖 Read it.

To be honest, it is true that April rains help flowers bloom in May.
It is good to be honest with your family and friends.

✏️ Write it in a sentence.

_____
_____

Name _____

Decodable Text

All about Flowers

Do you know the poem "April showers bring May flowers"? To be honest, it is true that April rains help flowers bloom in May. The flowers create a beautiful space!

Flowers come in many shapes and sizes. Some flowers are small, but some can be giant! They also come in many different shades, including neon. Flowers smell good and can make people feel happy. Some flowers even help clean our water and soil.

But watch out! Some flowers can be like poison if animals or humans eat them. But don't let that ruin the idea of flowers for you. Just be careful!

It is fun to get and give flowers. Flowers have the power to say things we can't put into words. Red roses can show love. Violets can tell a friend you are loyal and will be there for them. Green flowers can mean good luck. How would you react if someone brought you fresh flowers?

Not all flowers stand still all day. Certain flowers turn to face the sun. Some flowers trap and eat bugs. Other flowers are fast growing and grow up to a foot in just one day!

If you want to grow flowers at home, plant them in a sunny spot. Give them lots of space in the ground to grow. And keep the soil moist with fluids. Flowers do need showers to thrive!

▶ Draw a picture that shows what you read in the text.

Decodable Text

Name _____

Going Camping

If you are going camping for the first time, it may be best to go to a campground. A campground has safe places that are ringed with stones where you can build a fire. A campground might have water for cooking and washing. Some even have cabins with indoor showers and power for using lights at night.

Lots of people enjoy camping. If they like a campground, they may come back year after year as loyal customers of the same place. Some campgrounds give discounts to honor repeat campers.

People who go camping likely enjoy being outside in the fresh air. While camping, they may have cookouts two or three times a day. They may enjoy hiking in the woods or boating on a lake or river. Some people like to camp because it makes them think of camping trips they took when they were young.

If you do go camping, keep the campground clean and follow safety rules. Put out your fire each night. A fire could destroy the beautiful campground. Pick up all your trash. The next people who camp there will thank you.

▶ Draw a picture that shows what you read in the text.

Name _____

Silent Letter Combinations

Phonics

Some graphemes are called silent letter combinations. In a silent letter combination, we say the sound of only one letter, and the other letter is silent.

Some silent letter combinations include: *kn* /n/, *gn* /n/, *lm* /m/, *mb* /m/, *gh* /g/, and *wr* /r/.

▶ Write each word in the correct box.

Word Bank

ghee
wreath
gnat
lamb
gherkin
palm
knight
ghost
climb
wreck
ghoul
knock
calm
wrist
gnash
write

Words with /n/	**Words with /m/**
_____	_____
_____	_____
_____	_____
_____	_____

Words with /g/	**Words with /r/**
_____	_____
_____	_____
_____	_____
_____	_____

Grade 2   Module 12 • Week 1

Name _____

Digraph ch /k/, /sh/

We already know the digraph *ch* can stand for the /ch/ sound, as in *cheetah*.

The digraph *ch* can also stand for the /k/ sound, as in *chorus*, and for the /sh/ sound, as in *chef*.

▶ Read each clue. Unscramble the tiles. Write the word correctly on the line.

Word Bank

chef   chick   chute   child   charades   ache   chrome   school

1. A little boy or girl | d | i | l | ch | _____

2. Someone who cooks | f | ch | e | _____

3. Where we learn | oo | s | ch | l | _____

4. An acting game | de | ch | s | ar | a | _____

5. A baby bird | i | ch | ck | _____

6. Another word for hurt | che | a | _____

7. A slide | te | ch | u | _____

8. A bright silver | ch | me | r | o | _____

Phonics Review

In a silent letter combination, we say the sound of only one letter. The graphemes *kn, gn, lm, mb, gh,* and *wr* are all silent letter combinations.

The digraph *ch* can stand for three different sounds: /ch/ as in *cheetah,* /k/ as in *chorus,* and /sh/ as in *chef.*

▶ Write the word that names the picture.

Irregular Words

Name _____

Read and Spell

Read and spell this word to be a better reader.

📖 Read it.

tough

👆 Tap the sounds.

○ ○ ○ ○ ○ ○ ○

✏️ Color it by sound.

tough

✏️ Write it.

_____

✏️ Write it again.

_____

📖 Read it.

This was a tough problem.

Sometimes telling who is who can be tough.

✏️ Write it in a sentence.

_____

_____

Grade 2   312   Module 12 • Week 1
© Houghton Mifflin Harcourt Publishing Company. All rights reserved.

Name _____

Irregular Words

Read and Spell

Read and spell this word to be a better reader.

📖 **Read it.**

rough

✋ **Tap the sounds.**

◯ ◯ ◯ ◯ ◯ ◯ ◯

✏️ **Color it by sound.**

rough

✏️ **Write it.**

_____

✏️ **Write it again.**

_____

📖 **Read it.**

She was having a rough time.

The fabric was rough and hard to cut.

✏️ **Write it in a sentence.**

_____

_____

Grade 2   312a   Module 12 • Week 1

Irregular Words

Name _____

Read and Spell

Read and spell this word to be a better reader.

 Read it.

enough

 Tap the sounds.

○ ○ ○ ○ ○ ○ ○

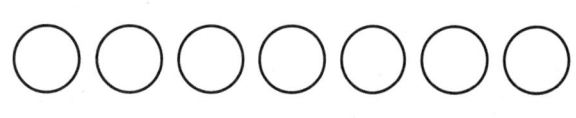 Color it by sound.

enough

 Write it.

_____

Write it again.

_____

Read it.

Then the lamb yawned because she had enough.

I think I have had enough pickles for now.

Write it in a sentence.

_____

_____

Name _____

Decodable Text

A Knock at the Door

Prem was making dinner in the kitchen. Rin was knitting a blanket for her friend Danna. Danna was going to have a baby very soon. The blanket had a design of little gnomes around the edges. Rin hoped Danna would like it.

Rin could hear a knocking sound. She thought it was Prem banging pots and pans in the kitchen, but when he asked if she could get it, she knew that someone was at the door.

Rin was surprised to see Danna standing there with a knapsack. Danna told Rin and Prem that a pipe had burst, and her home was flooded. She was having a rough time and asked if she could sleep at Prem and Rin's that night.

Rin and Prem were happy to have Danna spend the night at their place. Danna saw Rin's knitting and smiled. "Is that for the baby?" she asked. "It's so cute!"

Rin had wanted the blanket to be a surprise, but she was glad Danna liked it. She went to get a plate, knife, fork, and spoon to set a place at the table for Danna.

There would be three for dinner that night.

▶ Draw a picture that shows what you read in the text.

Decodable Text

Name _____

My Tiny Lamb

I have a tiny pet lamb. She fits in the curve of my hand. When she gets sleepy, she naps on my thumb. In her calm voice, she tells me things she wants.

One day she said, "I want oats." So I fed her oats, crumb by crumb.

One day she said, "I want to comb my wool." So I got her a tiny comb.

Then she said, "I want to climb an elm tree."

This was a tough problem. An elm tree was way too big for her to climb.

But then it came to me. I snapped a twig from the limb of a tree. I stuck it in the ground. I watched the lamb climb up. I watched the lamb climb down. She went up and down her twig ten times. Then the lamb yawned because she had enough. She took an extra long nap in my palm.

▶ Draw a picture that shows what you read in the text.

Name _____

Decodable Text

The Write Story

Grandma sat on the couch and looked at a globe of the world. Her grandson, Lawrence, was in the kitchen. He knocked on the lid of a jar of pickles. Then he wrenched the lid off and shouted to Grandma, "Would you like another gherkin?"

Grandma wrinkled her nose. "Thank you, Lawrence. I think I have had enough pickles for now."

Lawrence sat next to Grandma and spun the globe. Then he put his finger on a spot, and the globe stopped spinning. "Can you tell me about this place?" he asked.

"I can," Grandma said, "because I used to live there. That is the country of Ghana."

"Wow, Grandma! You used to live in Ghana?" said Lawrence.

"I did," she said. "That is where my family is from. We lived there until I was thirteen."

Lawrence was amazed. He sat and listened as Grandma told her story of living in Ghana, moving to the United States, and growing older.

"And that's when I was born," Lawrence said at the end.

"You are not wrong," Grandma said with the ghost of a smile. "And what happens next? That part of the story is up to you to write. Now, let's have another gherkin."

▶ Draw a picture that shows what you read in the text.

Decodable Text

Name _____

Triple Talent

Jude, Mabel, and Dean are triplets with the same big smile and the same dark, curly hair. They are in the same class and often dress the same. They even like to eat the same foods. Sometimes telling who is who can be tough and then it causes chaos. But friends know that they like to do different things.

Jude is funny and loves playing jokes on his friends. He sometimes wears a fake mustache and moves like a robotic machine. Jude likes to mix things up and wants to work in a lab as a chemist when he grows up.

Mabel loves all kinds of music. She is in the school chorus and can reach high notes with ease. Mabel takes music lessons on the weekend and can play beautiful chords on her harp. But Mabel dreams of playing drums in a rock band one day.

Dean spends his time in the kitchen. He can cook a four-course meal from scratch. And he bakes the best pies and tarts you've ever tasted. Dean wants to be a master chef and teach others how to cook.

Do you know any triplets or twins? How are they alike? How are they different?

▶ Draw a picture that shows what you read in the text.

Name _____

Phonics

Prefix un-

A prefix is a word part added to the beginning of a base word to change its meaning. The prefix *un–* means "not" or "opposite." The word *unhappy* begins with the prefix *un–* and means "not happy." The word *unlock* begins with the prefix *un–*. To *unlock* something is the opposite of locking something.

▶ Choose and write a word to complete each sentence. Use each word once.

Word Bank

unwell   unlock   unhappy   untie   unpack   unfair

1. Drew had to _____ the door with her key.

2. I think the rules he made up are _____ .

3. I was feeling _____ after eating the food.

4. Can you help me _____ my sneaker?

5. We help my dad _____ the groceries from the store.

6. I was _____ that my dog chewed my toy.

Name _____

Phonics

Prefixes re-, pre-

A prefix is a syllable added to the beginning of a word to change its meaning. Examples: *pre-* means "before," *re-* means "again."

▶ Add a prefix to the word in dark print to complete each sentence. Use these prefixes: *pre-* or *re-*.

1. Marco wants to **heat** up a pizza in the oven.

   Marco will need to _____ the oven first so that it gets hot.

2. Can you **tell** me the story?

   I can't wait to _____ that story to my sister!

3. I like to **play** a song while I do my chores.

   Sometimes, I even keep it on _____ and listen to it over and over!

4. Paul **drew** a cartoon for the school paper.

   Paul _____ the cartoon because he ripped it.

5. My grandpa and I **made** an apple pie.

   We used a _____ crust, but the filling was homemade!

6. I go to **school** every day.

   My little sister goes to _____ since she is not old enough for big school yet.

Grade 2 — 315 — Module 12 • Week 2

Name _____

Phonics

Phonics Review

You can add a **prefix** to the beginning of a base word to change the word's meaning. Some prefixes are un–, re–, and pre–.

un + happy = unhappy   re + tell = retell
pre + heat = preheat

▶ Add the correct prefix to each base word to complete the sentence.

1. Hal will _____ **read** the book.

2. Please _____ **tangle** my laces.

3. Dad needs to _____ **heat** the oven to make dinner.

4. She will _____ **paint** the room.

5. Can you _____ **lock** the door?

6. We took a _____ **test** to see what we already knew.

7. Julia can _____ **play** the movie.

8. Mom will _____ **zip** her bag.

9. My _____ **teen** sister just turned twelve.

Name _____

Decodable Text

A Change of Plans

Ana had traveled far on her trip. She was in a new town and wanted to rest. She went to the room she would be staying in and unpacked her bags. She plugged in her phone to charge it. She unwrapped the scarf from her neck and took off her coat and boots.

She wanted to stay in that day to rest from her long train ride. She ordered hot tea and a sandwich and finished unpacking her suitcase while she waited for the food.

When her food came, Ana unwrapped the sandwich and poured a cup of tea. Then her phone rang. It was the friend she had come to see. Ana unplugged her phone and brought it to the table.

Her friend wanted to meet her in town. The town was having a fair. Her friend wanted Ana to see it.

Ana ate her food and drank her tea. She put her coat, scarf, and boots back on. She was going to see her friend and go to the fair. She could rest later. She was having a great trip!

▶ Draw a picture that shows what you read in the text.

Name _____

Decodable Text

A Retelling

It was a story that had been told lots of times. The class was going to rewrite it and put their own spin on it.

In the story, someone does a good deed, and the person who gains from this deed wants to repay the person who did the good deed. The problem was that the person who did the good deed did not want anyone to know who she was. She requested that no one tell about her act.

So the person who gained from the good deed tried to retrace the mystery woman's steps. He reread the note that explained the deed and looked for a return address.

He rode from town to town to ask about a person who did good deeds. He thought he might as well do some good deeds while he was on the road. The people he met thanked him, and that made him feel good.

He never did find the mystery woman, but in a way, he had repaid her kind act with good deeds of his own.

The class rewrote the tale, and then they acted it out for the rest of the school.

▶ Draw a picture that shows what you read in the text.

Name _____

Decodable Text

Pregame Party

The Bears hockey team had been training hard, and their first game of the term was coming up. The three coaches for the Bears wanted to throw a party to thank the team for their hard work. The coaches took time to preplan the food and drinks they would prepare for the team.

They precut fruit into slices and preheated the grill to cook some of the party food. There was potato salad and green salad as well as hot dogs and burgers to cook on the grill. When the food was ready, they set the table, put on music, and waited for the team to arrive.

All the team members came, and everyone had a great time at the party. After everyone ate, they danced and played a bunch of fun games together. The party was a big success!

The team members helped clean up when the party was over. They thanked their coaches for having them. And they hoped their hockey term would be as great as the party!

▶ Draw a picture that shows what you read in the text.

Name _____

Phonics

Prefix in-

A prefix is a syllable, or word part, added to the beginning of a word to change its meaning. The prefix *in-* adds the meaning "not" or "opposite." The word *incomplete* has the prefix *in-* and means "not complete."

▶ Choose and write a word to complete each sentence. Use each word once.

Word Bank

invisible   incomplete   invalid   inexpensive   inactive   independent

1. If I had a superpower, I would want to be _____ !

2. It is important to learn how to be _____ as you get older.

3. The test results were _____ because of a mistake on the form.

4. We like to eat here because the food is _____ but very good!

5. If you do not move around a lot, you might be called _____ .

6. I've been writing a book, but it is _____ since I'm not finished yet.

Name _____

Phonics

Prefixes dis- and mis-

The prefix *dis–* means "not" or "opposite" and can also mean "apart" or "away." The word *dislike* means to not like something. The word *disconnect* means to take away the connection.

The prefix *mis–* means "wrong" or "badly." The word *misspell* means to spell a word wrong.

▶ Add a prefix to the word in dark print to complete each sentence. Use these prefixes: *dis–* or *mis–*.

1. Matt **counted** the cups and plates for the party.

   He _____ and had to count them again.

2. Ann **deals** seven cards to each player.

   She _____ and gives Dan only six cards.

3. Chan **likes** apples and bananas.

   She _____ candy that tastes like apples or bananas.

4. Benny **matched** all the clean socks for Mom.

   He _____ a dark blue sock with a black sock.

5. Mario **connected** his tablet to the charger.

   When it was fully charged, he _____ his tablet from the charger.

Name _____

Phonics Review

A prefix is a word part added to the beginning of a base word to change its meaning. Examples: *in–* = "not" or "opposite;" *dis–* = "not," "opposite," "apart," "away;" *mis–* = "wrong" or "badly"

▶ Choose a word from the box to complete each sentence. Use each word once.

Word Bank

| mistake | displeased | misspelled |
| incomplete | disconnected | independently |

1. Alex looked over his work _____ .

2. He saw a _____ word on the last page.

3. Alex was _____ with himself.

4. He did not want to turn in work with a _____ .

5. Alex fixed the spelling and turned in his paper so that it was not _____ .

6. He _____ his laptop and sat quietly at his desk.

Name _____

Decodable Text

First Things First

The kids got an early start in the morning. Inside, they put on outfits for the outside yard work. Sometimes Mom was indirect, but today she made it clear—first a yard cleanup and then swimming.

Each kid had a job to do. Even the littlest ones joined in doing their part. They worked together in the garden. Mom wanted the weeds to be invisible.

Mom got each kid's input. The oldest boy wanted to mow the lawn. He knew that there was a correct and an incorrect way to do this job. Mom showed him how to mow in neat rows and trim around the trees.

The sun got hotter and hotter as the day went on. The kids worked hard and had sweat and dirt from head to toe. Mom knew they needed to cool off.

"We spend enough time indoors, so it was nice to be outside today," said Mom. "Thank you all for helping. Now it is time for swimming! Who is going to be the first one to jump in?"

▶ Draw a picture that shows what you read in the text.

Name _____

Disconnect at the Pool

Did you do a lot of hard work this year? Is it time to disconnect your brain? Join us at the pool this summer! A daily swim will cool your body and relax your mind.

You may ask: What if I don't swim well? What if I dislike pools? Our swimming experts will help you. We will not rest until you can float on your own and swim with ease.

Our pool is a safe place. You will find that our pool is sparkling clean. We disinfect it each day! We also display some rules. There is no running around the pool or diving into the shallow end. Swimmers must keep their hands and feet to themselves. And disrespect is not allowed. Those who disobey the rules will be asked to leave.

If you are displeased with the pool, please speak with one of our staff members! Our goal is to make your summer dreams come true.

▶ Draw a picture that shows what you read in the text.

Name _____

Decodable Text

Lost and Found

Yikes! The bus is waiting and you can't find your backpack. We've all made the mistake of misplacing things—books, toys, keys, wallets, and even cars!

Wouldn't it be great if we had a tool to help us find our things? Well, the good news is that there is such a thing today! It is called a GPS tag or tracker.

GPS tags and trackers come in different shapes and sizes. You can buy a tracker and place it on an item you want to be able to find if you misplace it, such as the TV remote. The tracker is connected to a mobile device. When you cannot find the item, you open an app on the device and tap on the name of the item. The tracker rings loudly and shows where the item is on a map.

Do not be misled. Some trackers can only find things close by, while others are able to find things far, far away. You can go online and read about how each kind of tracker works, so you are not misinformed.

You may even want to find out if there is a tracker that can locate misplaced homework!

▶ Draw a picture that shows what you read in the text.